T0199091

Dr Ben Quartsin

ARISE

Break Free from the Tyranny of Your Past: Your New Life Starts Now

WESTBOW
PRESS®
A DIVISION OF THOMAS NELSON
& ZONDERVAN

Copyright © 2020 Dr Ben Quartsin.

All rights reserved. No part of this book may be used or reproduced by any means, graphic, electronic, or mechanical, including photocopying, recording, taping or by any information storage retrieval system without the written permission of the author except in the case of brief quotations embodied in critical articles and reviews.

WestBow Press books may be ordered through booksellers or by contacting:

WestBow Press
A Division of Thomas Nelson & Zondervan
1663 Liberty Drive
Bloomington, IN 47403
www.westbowpress.com
1 (866) 928-1240

Because of the dynamic nature of the Internet, any web addresses or links contained in this book may have changed since publication and may no longer be valid. The views expressed in this work are solely those of the author and do not necessarily reflect the views of the publisher, and the publisher hereby disclaims any responsibility for them.

Any people depicted in stock imagery provided by Getty Images are models, and such images are being used for illustrative purposes only. Certain stock imagery © Getty Images.

Scriptures taken from the Holy Bible, New International Version®, NIV®. Copyright © 1973, 1978, 1984, 2011 by Biblica, Inc.™ Used by permission of Zondervan. All rights reserved worldwide. www.zondervan.com The "NIV" and "New International Version" are trademarks registered in the United States Patent and Trademark Office by Biblica, Inc.™

Scripture taken from the New King James Version®. Copyright © 1982 by Thomas Nelson. Used by permission. All rights reserved.

ISBN: 978-1-9736-6027-9 (sc)
ISBN: 978-1-9736-6026-2 (hc)
ISBN: 978-1-9736-6028-6 (e)

Library of Congress Control Number: 2019904405

Print information available on the last page.

WestBow Press rev. date: 1/10/2020

Contents

Acknowledgements

I'd like to thank all the people without whom this book would not have been written. Firstly I'd like to thank my wife, as I wouldn't have found the time to write without her help and support, and my mother for her foresight in seeking that her children achieve more than herself.

I also extend my sincere thanks to my two friends Bright Okine and Aaron Njagi, who both worked tirelessly to help shape the contents of this book. Additionally, I wish to express my gratitude to Dr Sunday Adelaja for his continued mentorship and for the numerous books of his that have helped guide my thoughts. Finally, I want to honour the memory of Dr Myles Munroe, whose book, *The Pursuit of Purpose* inspired some of the topics here.

Preface

At 25, I had an idea of how my future would look. I didn't have all the details, but I knew the direction it should take. Every day, I dreamed about my aspirations.

Then life happened: I took a couple of turns, and before I knew it, all my dreams had dissolved into nothing. Several years of living without dreams went by. I didn't go off the rails or anything, and many of the people I knew would have said that I was living a meaningful life. In fact, during this time, I completed postgraduate training and started working as a Consultant Psychiatrist. I raised a family, worked hard, paid my bills, and liked to think that I'd helped a few people.

For a while, that seemed enough, but then I began to sense that something was missing. I looked for answers, but none seemed to be forthcoming. A year into this search for answers, someone sent me a video of a man who would later become my mentor. The things he shared in this video were revolutionary. I had never heard anyone say that "life is predictable", and yet this is what he seemed to be saying.

Most of the people I knew at the time would have disagreed with that statement, saying that no one knows what the future holds. But there was such certainty in this man's voice and his words made so much sense that I decided to check him out. He was hosting a training programme a few weeks later, so I decided to go and meet him. It turned out to be one of the best decisions I've ever made.

I've been on a few personal development courses in my time, but none of them come close to the one I experienced in Kiev. There was not a word said about time management, and yet I came back with a bag load of ideas on how to manage my time better. Most importantly, I found answers to the questions I'd been asking. Not only did I return from Ukraine with a clear purpose, but what was even better, I started dreaming again.

My experience in Kiev sparked in me a keen desire not only to live my life more purposefully, but it also gave me the drive to help others do the same. And that's the reason for writing this book. In many respects, it's a personal guide for me that I also wish to share, if, peradventure, it will help someone.

As you read it, I sincerely hope that you too will rediscover your purpose. I also hope you'll start dreaming again—that's the greatest thing that could ever happen to you!

Foreword

I've read this book several times now, and each time I read it, I feel as though I had written it myself. That's because the content resonates so much with my own thoughts. It's truly remarkable!

What great encouragement this book offers—it will certainly be a source of hope to anyone who is unhappy with the status quo and wishes to start making the most of their lives.

"Hope at last!" is really the message of the book, and the author knows exactly what this means, having overcome his own big challenges and taken a giant step towards his destiny.

I can't help but marvel at the determination and dedication with which he has approached this writing while working full-time as a doctor.

I would like to recommend the book to anyone serious about turning their lives around. I can say this with confidence because I've personally seen the principles the author presents here bear fruit in his own life. This is not a collection of good ideas but rather one of well-proven principles to help you make the most of your life.

With Arise, your wasted life and lack of purpose will change as you begin to embrace a life of purpose and vision, and a life geared towards contributing your share in making the world a better place for everybody and for the Kingdom of God.

Kudos to you Dr Quartsin! Keep them coming and leave a legacy.

For the love of God, Church and Nation,

Dr Sunday Adelaja
Embassy of God Church

Awaken that sleeping giant in you and create a brighter future!

Each person walking on the face of this planet holds potential that is yet to be tapped. This fact is as true of the pauper as it is of the king—each one of us is like a mighty oak tree waiting to bud. But as Rob Moore puts it in his book, *Start Now Get Perfect Later*, we're all Jedi Masters at sabotaging our own destinies. We desire one thing but end up pursuing something else. We accumulate philosophies that have nothing to do with where we want to be in life, and they end up tripping us up. We beat ourselves up about our mistakes but never let go, and worst of all, we stumble through life never bothering to find out what we're actually here for. And as a consequence, we fail to fulfil our potential.

As an acorn remains but a seed until it falls into the ground, so our potential remains unfulfilled until we discover the "soil" within which *we* can flourish. This book discusses these issues and more. It highlights the common mistakes we all make and suggests ways to leave them behind and create the kind of life we crave.

The book is really divided into two parts. The first four chapters are designed to stir up discontent and generate an appetite for change. The author does this by bringing you face-to-face with your mistakes, failures and missed opportunities. The second part, from Chapter 5 onward, is designed to give you the tools for change.

To make the most of the content, it's a good idea to first read right through the book, highlighting the parts that catch your attention. You should then re-read it focusing on the sections that speak to you, and highlighting anything else that stands out.

Allow yourself time to think. Go to a quiet place or maybe go for a walk, and think deeply about your life. Don't put the book down until you've made some decisions, but don't rush into making any big changes straightaway. Try instead to understand what the changes will involve, then make a plan to achieve your goal. If you manage to change one small thing in your life, this effort will have been worthwhile.

Chapter 1

The crisis

Prison officer:	"All right then, Sarah, that's your cell. How long have you got this time?"Asks the officer with the hint of disdain that Sarah is all too familiar with.
Sarah:	"I haven't been to court yet."
Prison officer:	"Remand?"
Sarah:	"Yes."
Prison officer:	"What's it this time? Burglary, theft, drugs?"
Sarah:	"I don't want to talk about it."

Stepping into her cell, Sarah experiences that familiar feeling flooding in. When will all this end? She wonders. Having been through it all before, she'd hoped it wouldn't happen again, but here she is, only a year later, in the same situation.

Born in rather unfortunate circumstances, Sarah was the result of an unwanted pregnancy—neither parent had wanted a child. They met at a nightclub, one thing led to another, and Sarah's mother, Amy, got pregnant. Many urged Amy to abort the baby, but it didn't seem the right thing to do. Sarah's father deserted Amy not long after the baby was born, so it was a long struggle as a single mother. She'd be the first to admit that she'd made a hash of parenting, but what else could she have done? She knew no better. Her mother abandoned her as a child, and her life was a long chain of foster homes, as she struggled to settle in any one. Who was there to teach her that introducing your own child to drugs is a bad idea?

By the age of 13, Sarah was hooked on pot, and would regularly smoke it with her mother. Life was tough. There was little money for food, and the bills often went unpaid, so Amy taught her daughter a few "tricks".

Amy had served a few prison sentences herself, and Sarah followed in her footsteps, but she hates herself for it. Deep down, she aspires to be different. She has sometimes thought about training to be a nurse like a lady she once saw in a documentary. She'd also like to have a family with maybe two kids—not more. Sarah has even thought about names for them. If only she could break free from this web, she seems to have been caught in.

Ten miles away, at the other side of town, is Andy. He is also in a pensive mood. He's felt the same for the past few months, maybe even longer, although his life has been very different from Sarah's. He has no criminal history for one thing—not even a parking offence. He hasn't suffered any real hardships either; on the contrary, many would say he's had an easy life. As an only child, he was spoiled rotten. He went on exotic holidays with his family and got every present he ever wanted. Christmas and birthdays were always wonderful, and with both parents coming from rather large families, there was never a shortage of aunties and uncles trying to outdo each other with their presents. By his seventh birthday, he had all the things that many children could only dream of: bikes, computers, video games, and even a horse, although he could barely ride it.

Andy's parents had to wait a long time to have him, so his arrival was a big deal. And since they believed in planning, they went to work as soon as they knew he was on the way. They planned everything, including the décor of his room, the clothes he would wear, the schools he would attend, and even the kind of career he would follow. They weren't going to leave anything to chance.

As soon as Andy was born, his parents went about executing their plan. They enrolled him in a private school where, in addition to the main curriculum, he'd have the opportunity to do things that children in state schools would never have the chance of doing. He learned to ride a horse when he was ten, and as captain of the cricket club, he'd travelled the world by the time he was sixteen.

After studying engineering at university, Andy landed a job straight away. Starting out in a junior position, he rose through the ranks to become the middle-grade manager he is today. The salary is great, and the job comes with quite a few perks including a good pension. Andy's colleagues like him, and he is generally well-respected at work.

It's a similar story at home. Andy has two children, both in their teens, and a lovely wife who is very supportive. Everything seems hunky-dory; yet Andy isn't happy.

For the past couple of years, he's been feeling bored. He comes home from work, has a meal, slumps on the sofa, and before long, he's fast asleep. Life has become rather mundane. Everything seems fine at work; he manages to get through the workday without problems, but the interest and desire have gone.

It may sound strange, but these two individuals with vastly different life trajectories are actually in a similar place. They're both sensing the need for change. Oddly enough, Sarah is in a better position because she understands what's wrong and knows the changes she'd like to make in her life. Andy, on the other hand, isn't quite sure of what needs to change. He just knows that he cannot continue like this for any longer. And that's how many people feel today. They've reached the point where they no longer want to continue on the same path, but have no clue which way to turn. They seem to have exhausted their ideas on how to live. Could they be experiencing a midlife crisis?

Why it happens

The term *midlife crisis* was coined by Elliot Jacques, a Canadian psychoanalyst, to describe the challenges that many adults face as they transition from young adulthood into older adulthood. Based on observations from his psychoanalytic practice and perhaps also from his own life, Jacques concluded that when people are confronted with their mortality as they grow older, it triggers a range of behaviours that could be described as a race against time. Some become preoccupied with their health and physical appearance, while others play catchup with their dreams or try to right some of the wrongs in their lives.

Jacques's views quickly found support among certain psychologists. His theory helped explain behaviours commonly observed in midlife like sexual flings and facelifts, but others argued that what he referred to as a "crisis" was not experienced across the board and that it was for some people a natural phase of life. And recent studies seem to confirm that—no definitive period corresponding to a "midlife crisis" has been found. So for some, there's no such thing as a "midlife crisis".

But it seems to me that in our quest to disprove his theory, we've missed the point Jacques seemed to be making. During the midlife period, people often feel they're at a crossroads. This realisation may force us to pause and reflect on our lives, and we may well end up on a different trajectory as a result.

I've seen boisterous and assertive people turn timid and introverted in midlife. They weren't ill; nor had they experienced any catastrophic life event. These individuals had become more aware of the fast-changing pace of life around them and seen others taking strides forward while they themselves remained stuck in their difficulties. Realising that things would only get worse with age, these sufferers, unable to find any answers, withdrew into their shells. When they were younger, they could hope that their finances and other aspects of their life would improve with time, but now in their forties, a dramatic change in their fortunes looked a lot less likely.

I've also observed people undergo profound changes in their personality and outlook on life upon retirement or following bereavement or a health scare. I've seen selfish and uncaring people turn sober and sensitive to the needs of others after a cancer diagnosis, for example. And these observations have led me to the conclusion that Jacques was onto something. There's a reason for these changes to occur at certain transition points. Whether you want to call it a crisis or not is another matter.

The reason for a drastic change of approach to life after a health scare seems obvious. A confrontation with our mortality often does a lot to sober the mind. And as for someone becoming more pensive in retirement, no longer having a job to get up for—after years of relying on work for structure and meaning—the explanation seems obvious.

But there's another factor involved here that is perhaps more significant. Having more time on your hands during retirement naturally leads to greater introspection. It is at this time that we'll all be forced to ponder how we've lived our lives. Strangely, midlife seems to entail a similar experience.

By midlife, most of us find that our children are in their teens and have become more independent. In many cases, they can barely tolerate our presence, whereas they might have demanded our undivided attention when they were younger. Finding that we have more time on our hands than usual, like the pensioner, we may be forced to stop and reflect.

This is Andy's situation. Life for him has slowed right down. The children, who once scrambled for his attention are now caught up in their own worlds. When Andy arrives home from work, they are often in their rooms chatting with friends or doing their homework. At the same time, things have gone a bit flat between him and his wife, Gemma, so Andy often finds himself alone without much to do, and this makes him think a lot more. But will he realise that this downtime he's experiencing is a signal from his inner self to focus on an appraisal?

Everyone needs a checkup

In the corporate world, employees undergo yearly appraisals. The appraisal is a chance for both the employer and the employee to take stock. For the employee, it's an opportunity to reflect on how well they've performed in the previous year, and in what areas improvements are still needed. The employer, on the other hand, gets to learn about any challenges the employee may be facing, and can provide support structures where necessary.

But appraisals aren't limited to the workplace. Shopkeepers, for instance, regularly check their stock to identify the goods that aren't selling well, and avoid stocking up on goods that few customers purchase.

Students, on the other hand, attend review meetings with their tutors. Such meetings provide a safe space to discuss progress along with any challenges the student may be facing. These meetings can be as important as the lessons and exams. Problems such as a lack of confidence, bullying, inattention and bad behaviour could all be discussed and addressed before they start affecting the student's grades.

Likewise, our lives require regular appraisals. We need to check whether our actions match our intentions and whether we're on the right track for achieving our goals. The appraisal will show us if we've strayed off course, and need to get ourselves back on track. But not many of us actually plan our lives like this. Instead, we tend to muddle our way through things without setting goals, and when we do set them, we often have no mechanisms for ensuring that we're achieving these goals. We get caught up in the rat race chasing the next thing in front of us until life slows down, perhaps in midlife. At this point, we begin to understand our lack of progress, and we're finally forced into doing the appraisal we've been avoiding.

In midlife, whether or not we deserve this opportunity, having missed so many others along the way, life offers a transition period for us to pause and reflect if we recognise the need to do so. Sadly, not many of us do realise this. We worry about the wrinkles on our faces instead and go for a facial, a tummy tuck or a hair transplant in an unconscious bid to slow down the passage of time. And the adventurous among us try our hands at an extreme sport, almost as though to prove to ourselves that we're not past it.

We purchase our dream cars, motorbikes or expensive gadgets; maybe embarking on that dream holiday, and there's nothing wrong with that. We feel nostalgic and organise reunions, and find new pursuits to fill all the free time we may now have in midlife. But we fail to do the one thing that life seems to call us to do, just as Andy is in danger of doing.

With each day that passes, Andy looks increasingly forlorn. Meanwhile, Gemma is worried that he might be suffering from depression. Chatting with her best friend Tracey, Gemma learns that Tracey's husband Craig had been through a similar period of melancholy. Since buying an expensive new bike, he's been out riding with friends and seems to have his mojo back. Gemma wonders whether this solution would work for Andy too, and thinks about getting him a bike for his birthday, but Andy doesn't want a bike. He knows that a new hobby pursuit will not dispel his discontentment. And he's right. What he's experiencing isn't merely a phase of life, or a storm that needs to be weathered until it subsides and is forgotten. A voice from deep within is telling Andy to sit down and appraise his life. Unless he heeds this voice, he'll soon find himself drifting into an even deeper crisis.

Chapter 2

Feeling stuck? Take stock!

If you're like Sarah, you'll often have days like the ones she's having now in prison. The consequences of your past mistakes are a constant reminder that something isn't quite right, and this awareness forces you to frequently evaluate your life. And yet, your assessments may not reveal very much or help you to change.

Sarah knows more than anyone just how badly she needs to change. The road she's travelling on is heading towards disaster. That much she knows. She's also clear about the kind of future she wants, but the path to her dreams seems a tortuous one, and so far, her attempts to follow it have failed.

She tried enrolling in a college, but that didn't go very well. As had often happened before, she got into an argument with one of the other students, things got a little heated, and she was asked to leave. Needless to say, her countless attempts to give up drugs and alcohol have failed each time.

Sarah seems to be caught in a trap from which there's no escape, and yet, the only reason her attempts at self-rescue haven't succeeded is that she hasn't quite understood her predicament.

She's aware of her need for education, but oblivious of her need to be schooled. She wants to be free from crime and drugs, but hasn't quite understood the factors keeping her reliant on them, or how she could break free. Sarah needs to do an appraisal, but of a different kind from the ones she's done so far. Instead of merely ruminating about her mistakes, she needs to critically examine her life. Just as a biologist dissects an organism and examines it under a microscope, so must she rise above her feelings of guilt and regret to view her mistakes more as case studies. She needs to study her past actions very carefully to clearly understand the reasons for her errors. Only then will she find lasting solutions. Sarah must aim to answer the following questions:

- Where am I?
- How did I get here?
- Where am I heading?
- Where do I want to be?
- How can I get there?

Where am I?

On the surface, the answer to the question of where Sarah is in life seems obvious. She's in prison, she has no qualifications, and she's never had a job. It looks pretty grim all around. But this question isn't merely about our social status or personal circumstances; it also relates to the kind of person we are, or more precisely, about the one we've become. Where we are in life is often not as tragic as the way life has affected us inwardly.

If you're in jail but have never identified with a criminal lifestyle, then your situation isn't as bad as it may seem. You may leave prison after you've served your sentence and never return. Life after prison could start to be good. But if you've developed a criminal perspective on life, then your best efforts to stay away from trouble may prove futile.

Sarah lacks many of the fundamentals that keep the majority of people away from the criminal justice system. She knows no alternative to street life. She could attempt drawing up yet another plan for her life, but it would be bound to fail because it would not take into account the person she has become.

When we plan our lives, we often do so with our best selves in mind. We stretch our imaginations and dream lofty dreams in the hope that we'll find the strength to make them come true. But we often forget where we are, and the tremendous effort it would take to get us out of the mess we're in. It's like someone sitting at the bottom of a pit, and drawing up elaborate plans for life outside the pit, but without having any idea of how to get out.

Sarah knows she has compassion for others, and believes she'd make a good nurse for this reason. But she must also acknowledge that this soft side lies buried deep inside her and must first be drawn out. She can't expect to achieve her dreams without first changing herself. If she attempts to reach her dream without first undergoing this process, she'll only end up sabotaging her own plans. Sarah must first have a plan for getting herself out of her pit. Only then can she achieve her dreams.

She needs a radical transformation in her body and soul. Sarah has been neglecting her other needs while focusing her efforts on obtaining her next fix, and her frequent cocaine use is damaging her body. She also needs a transformation in her soul. Whenever she has committed a crime and gone through the criminal justice system, she has unknowingly subjected her soul to abuse. Sarah can only break free from this cycle when she fully acknowledges her problems, and all the changes she needs to make.

How did I get here?

Life is like a road trip. The destination is your goal. To reach it, you need to know the route and keep moving forward. At the same time, the ability to visualise your future will enable you to fulfil your purpose, and your enthusiasm and determination will ensure that you never take your foot off the pedal.

To travel safely on the road, you need to stay in the right lane. In life, this equates to carefully minding your own business. Equally, you have to stay alert to avoid collisions with other drivers who—not watching where they're going—might stray into your lane. The collisions are the arguments, fights or disputes that can send us off-course so easily.

You need to develop traits such as conscientiousness and self-discipline so you can abide by the highway code and avoid road rage incidents. In life, such traits help us to stay on course and avoid getting into trouble with the law.

You cannot afford to get overly excited on a road trip lest you miss your turning or take the wrong turning and become stranded. These errors correspond to our missed opportunities and mistakes. You need to learn how to negotiate the many traps and obstacles you'll come across in life, just as a driver skillfully manoeuvres his or her car around sharp bends.

Sarah's lack of self-discipline and poor self-control means she struggles to stay in her lane. This tendency has contributed to many of her troubles. Her most recent offence is one example.

On the way home from a nightclub, she and a friend popped into a corner shop for cigarettes. Sarah's friend got into an argument with the shopkeeper, who got upset and asked her to leave. Sarah wasn't involved in that exchange, but she didn't like the shopkeeper's tone, and as is often the case, she got drawn in.

An argument ensued, and before she knew it, she was all over him kicking, punching, and screaming. Her friend managed to drag her off the shopkeeper, but it was too late; someone had called the police.

Self-discipline allows us to stay on a task until we've completed it, and self-control helps us to ignore distractions. The two are closely-related concepts, and both are necessary for fulfilling our purpose. Without these abilities, we end up getting drawn into side issues, and in Sarah's case, fights.

Sarah needs to acquire these traits. She must also learn to distinguish between her goals and the distractions that abound in her environment. It is perhaps, admirable that she was willing to stick up for her friend, but her actions have resulted in her imprisonment and have diverted her from her plans. If she is to succeed in life, she must learn to give the right matters the right amount of attention, and pick her battles carefully, because not every battle is worth the effort even if we win it.

If you were taking part in a 100-metre race and heard someone shouting abuse from the stands, you'd have a choice. You could pick a fight with this person and talk some sense into them or simply carry on running. If you stop for a fight, you might win it, but you sure won't win the race. Sarah must decide what's more important, winning the little fights that life keeps throwing at her or pursuing her goal to achieve her dreams.

She needs to critically examine the incident mentioned above and any others that she's been involved in. This will help her identify the factors that have held sway over her decision making and prevented her from reaching her goals.

It's helpful to understand how the different aspects of ourselves, as outlined below, affect our decisions.

Values

Our values start forming from an early age, and our families, caregivers, peers and the education system all contribute to their formation. Having grown up on the streets, Sarah has missed out on forming the kind of values that keep most people from conflicts with the law. She knows right from wrong, but she lacks the inhibitions that a robust belief system brings, and so keeping her behaviour in check has been a challenge. While it's much easier to build values in childhood, it's actually never too late to do it. If she can understand the process, Sarah can begin to lay the foundation for a brighter future.

Self-esteem

This refers to the way we see ourselves. And how we view ourselves determines our view of our place in the world. Having low self-esteem means we give way to others even when we don't want to, and we fail to protest when our rights are trampled on. We also act as though we deserve the unfair treatment we receive from others. On the other hand, we might compensate for our low self-worth by becoming arrogant and aggressive.

Sarah has very low self-esteem. Not having achieved anything that she's set her mind on has left her feeling that nothing good will ever come of her life. Venturing into certain circles causes her anxiety. She's often fearful that she'll be exposed as a good-for-nothing illiterate, and is quick to draw inferences from other people's behaviour, which she interprets as demeaning. This habit has got her into many rows. If she's to make any progress with her life, she must first address her low self-esteem.

Temperament

Your temperament is your natural disposition; the combination of mental, physical and emotional traits responsible for the way you behave. Some people are quick to act, while others take a long time to make up their minds. Some get angry very quickly, while others keep their cool amid challenging circumstances. Sarah is often too quick to react, and this is the reason for some of the wrong choices she has made.

Mood

Some people's actions are simply the result of their feelings. On a good day, these types are kind and amiable, and easy to get along with. On a bad day...well, you probably wouldn't want to meet them then.

And because these types often feel very vulnerable, the smallest thing can cause a change in their mood, and this, of course, also affects their decisions. In some cases, such changeability is due to a medical condition, but moodiness with most people is nothing but a habit. Sarah needs to evaluate how her moods have influenced her decision making.

Relationships

We all value other people's opinions, and sometimes those opinions hold sway over our decisions. It's good when other people's views stop us from making bad choices. Children regulate their behaviour according to their parents' expectations. On the flip side though, someone else's opinions can also stop you from doing what you know to be right. I remember struggling with a career decision because I knew my boss wouldn't like it if he knew what I really wanted to do. That held me back for a while because I had a lot of respect for his views, but I eventually managed to get past this obstacle.

Sarah must be aware of the impact others have on her choices, and she needs to work hard to maximise the positive influences while limiting the negative ones. There are a few friends she could do without.

Knowledge

More often than not, our good decisions are a consequence of our having the right information. And by the same token, our regrettable choices are often the result of our ignorance of all the facts involved. Sarah's poor decisions are an indication that she's deficient in this area.

Habits

Bad habits can halt the pursuit of our dreams and sabotage our plans. As mentioned earlier, much of Sarah's energies have gone into her drug habit, and many of her problems have occurred when she's been intoxicated. To increase her chances of achieving her dreams, she first needs to address her alcohol and cocaine use.

Where am I heading?

It's often said that no one can predict the future, and there is some truth in that. But at the same time, it's important to understand that we *can*, with a fair degree of accuracy, predict how our lives will turn out if we continue along the same trajectory. If we regularly over-eat, for example; we can expect to be overweight in the future. If we keep spending more money than we actually have, we'll end up in a lot of debt. The future can be predicted with a fair amount of accuracy by the choices we make today, and the decisions we either take or neglect to take will set the tone for what will be.

Without a drastic change of mindset, Sarah will continue to break the law and keep returning to prison. If she's not careful, she may even end up committing a grave offence, and receive a lengthy jail term. This outcome would, of course, completely scupper all her plans.

Where do I need to be?

Sarah knows what she wants to do with her life, but she needs a clearer vision of the future that it may guide her. She also needs some mini-goals to help her progress towards her ultimate dream of becoming a nurse. We shall discuss this in more detail later.

How do I get there?

To change any problem area in our lives, we must first acknowledge the difficulty. We must also have a strong desire to change the unacceptable situation. Otherwise, we'll find that it's almost impossible to change a situation we've more-or-less accepted and can manage to tolerate. That's why breaking old habits is so hard.

Secondly, we need to understand the nature of the problem, and know how to effect the change. Finally, we must understand why this change is necessary. In other words, we need to answer what I've termed as the three most important questions in life: What? How? And Why? So far we've seen *why* Sarah cannot continue along the same path, and we've also outlined the areas that require a transformation. Now, we need to focus on *how* she can actually make the change.

Firming up

No one can build a house without first laying the foundation. As the foundation will support the entire building, any defect in the foundation will put the whole building at risk.

Everyone has a set of beliefs that form the foundation of their being. These beliefs shape and mould a person's actions, and determine their interactions with the outside world. Psychologists call them core beliefs.

A person's core beliefs are about the self, about others and about the world at large. These are all laid down in childhood. The love and warmth of our families and the consistency of the home environment enable us to form healthy views about ourselves; thereby shaping our interactions with others.

Sarah may not have had the chance to lay a solid foundation in childhood, but as we've explained already, it's not too late. If she can grasp the principles that govern the formation of core beliefs, she can start preparing the ground for a better future.

Firstly, she must be mindful of her environment. The people we surround ourselves with help to shape us, even though we might not know it. We embrace their ideals and internalise their preferences; sometimes even copying their mannerisms. If Sarah wants to change her life, she needs to surround herself with the kind of people who have the conduct she wants to emulate. To achieve this goal, she could join a church or a social group of some sort.

In a group, she can learn by observing and asking questions. Traits such as kindness and sensitivity to other people's suffering are acquired by direct observation and practice, and joining a group will help her to do that. She'll be able to see how others live their lives and learn how to live hers. And if she's lucky, she'll find a mentor, someone who'll take her under their wing and teach her the things she needs to know. She'll also get the opportunity to take on various roles, and if these involve caring for others, she can develop more sensitivity towards other people, along with a sense of responsibility.

Being part of a group will not only give Sarah a sense of belonging but will also enable her to become part of a community. She needs to know she matters to someone, and that someone is standing in the sidelines watching and cheering her on. Sarah needs a new family, as it were, and the right group may fulfil this need.

She may also get the chance to learn trust. Having grown up in a dog-eat-dog environment, she has naturally developed a distrust of others. Often suspicious of other people's intentions towards her, even when they mean no harm, Sarah's always on her guard. This attitude is her survival tactic. But the ability to trust is one of the keys to a happy life—and trust helps to bind society together. Sarah needs to learn to open up to people if she wants to play a meaningful role in society. Unless she does this, people will find it hard to trust her, and they're unlikely to offer her the opportunities she needs to improve herself. She must learn to relax her guard, but this can only be possible in an environment she feels safe in. It is therefore essential for Sarah to break free from her current social circle.

Sarah is also going to need an anchor. The desire to be a nurse is a good enough goal to keep anyone grounded, but with such powerful forces warring against her within her own soul, Sarah's goal will not be easy to realise. She needs someone or something she can rely on so she can stop drifting. For many, that anchor is friends and family, but Sarah, who lacks these assets, must look beyond her immediate environment for that anchor.

My anchor in life is my faith in God. This gives me a point of reference. I know where the boundaries are, and in times of trouble, I know where I can find solace. Having an anchor helps me to bounce back even when I've messed up. I can forgive myself and move on. Sarah needs an anchor too.

Back to school

The importance of education isn't lost on Sarah. She's aware that she'll need to get some qualifications if she is to fulfil her dreams. What she doesn't understand is that educational institutions don't only pass on knowledge, but they also help to shape behaviour. The restrictions and regimes that students are subjected to, mould them into responsible citizens and decent human beings.

School is where we learn to get along with others. By mixing with other children who are often very different from us, we become more accommodating. We also learn to respect others' views and keep our behaviour in check for their benefit. We learn to take responsibility through the roles that our teachers assign us.

School teaches us the value of time. The lessons take place over a fixed period, and the assignments and exams are all time-limited. This structure helps us to appreciate and manage time better. Sarah needs to take note of the benefits offered by educational institutions, and this will motivate her to persevere with the restrictions. So far, she's struggled to see any positives in going to school other than to obtain academic qualifications, so she needs to understand the other benefits too.

Another obstacle for Sarah is her struggle with the concept of authority. To her mind, authority figures do nothing but make your life difficult. From social workers who poke their noses in your business, to police officers who arrest you and throw you in jail, down to prison officers who tell you to keep quiet and behave yourself, when all you want is for someone to respond to your distress, Sarah's experience of authority has not been positive. But now she needs to bear in mind her ultimate goal and the dividends that submission could bring.

As a nurse, Sarah would be a member of a highly regulated profession with a hierarchical structure to which she would have to submit. She needs to start learning submission somewhere, and college is a good place to start. But she needs to go there with a different attitude. She should stop seeing school as something merely to be endured but go with a desire to learn instead.

All this means that Sarah's education will take place both inside and outside the classroom. In class, she'll learn self-discipline by applying herself to the tasks assigned. At the same time, by working collaboratively with her peers, she'll acquire teamworking skills. Meanwhile, having to get up each morning and head for lectures—even when she doesn't feel like it—will teach Sarah something about commitment. This is the kind of commitment she'll need when she starts working.

The cycle of change

Finally, Sarah needs to understand that change will take time. Making this kind of change in your life takes time because it will be a gradual process. It involves consistently focusing on the different areas involved over time, and the progress isn't necessarily constant— sometimes you'll succeed, sometimes you won't.

In 1983, two psychologists, James Prochaska and Carlo Di Clemente observed that change is not an event, as was previously thought, but a process involving stages. They proposed a model explaining that process, which has since been termed *the cycle of change*.

The first stage in this cycle is the *pre-contemplation stage* when the person still isn't quite ready to change. They're often not really aware of their problem, and if they are, they don't consider it as such. They may well laugh off any suggestion of the need to change, or even get annoyed. An alcoholic in the pre-contemplation stage will typically ask: "Why does everyone keep talking about my drinking?" The alcoholic doesn't consider it to be a problem.

Others in the pre-contemplation stage, are aware of their problems but so far, their attempts to address them have failed, leading to a feeling of disillusionment. Many people trying to lose weight are in this situation—they've registered with a gym or started a new diet—but have then struggled with motivation, and subsequently given up.

The most common reason for such failures is that people trying to lose weight, for example, have not tried to understand their problem before attempting to solve it. Although the benefits of weight loss may be clear, dieters often fail to understand the role food plays in their lives. For many, food is a comfort and a friend that helps them through the long wintry nights. For such people, going on a diet amounts to distancing themselves from what may be their sole source of comfort. It's hardly surprising that their attempts at weight loss should fail. To have any chance of succeeding, they need to realise the important role food plays in their lives, and also need to understand the price of change.

Sarah is in the pre-contemplation stage. Although she's aware of the need for change, and has already taken steps in that direction, she has hardly considered the kind of effort that's required. She's sure of the destination, but doesn't really know how to get there yet. To progress to the next phase in the cycle of change, she needs to think strategically and study her problems. Only then will she understand the depth of change that's needed.

The next stage is the *contemplation stage*. During this period, people are conscious of the benefits of change, but they're also aware of the difficulty in achieving it, which can sometimes leave them feeling daunted and unable to make a start. To break this impasse, it's necessary to see how the benefits of change will outweigh the cost. Sarah must appreciate not only the end result, that is, fulfilment of her dreams, but also the process itself and what it involves. Only then will she find the necessary motivation to begin the journey towards transformation. When this happens, she'll have propelled herself into the next stage in the cycle—the *preparation stage*.

A person in the preparation stage is mentally ready for change. They know what's involved, and can also see the path to their destination clearly. Now they need to identify the necessary measures to take to reach their goal.

Change doesn't happen just because we want it badly or believe it to be possible; it happens because we've prepared for it thoroughly. Sarah needs to be methodical about her transformation. She needs to draw up a plan, outlining her understanding of the challenges she's likely to face, and how to overcome them. Once she has the plan, she'll be ready to move to the *action stage*.

Sarah's plan will need to be executed in steps. As most of her criminal behaviour has been undertaken to fund her cocaine use, addressing this is going to be critical to any further progress. Luckily, she can start right where she is; she needn't wait until her release from prison. There's a Drug and Alcohol service within the prison that can help her overcome her addiction. She should first aim to understand the role drugs have played in her life, along with the factors that have kept her hooked.

It's crucial for Sarah to avoid the "Here I am; sort me out" mentality. Many people seeking to change are rather passive. They dump their problems on experts, expecting a quick fix, but true change only happens when we take ownership of the process. This is one of the reasons the 12-step programme employed by Alcoholics Anonymous and Narcotics Anonymous works. In this programme, participants are encouraged to take responsibility for their problems and take the lead in addressing them. Everyone who enrols in the programme gets a sponsor (mentor). Sponsors are fellow attendees who have achieved a measure of success in tackling their addiction, and who support their peers to do the same. They don't act like experts or take over the problems of the people they're sponsoring, and the good thing about this approach is that it forces the mentees to be fully engaged in the process of changing. This approach enhances their motivation and increases their chances of success. Sarah needs to embrace this approach, not only for her addiction but for her other problems as well. She needs to take full ownership.

She might want to join Narcotics Anonymous following her release from prison. This group could help her maintain any progress she makes in jail. At the meetings, she'll hear the others' stories about how they became drug addicts, and about the impact it has had on them and on their loved ones. The more she learns about other people's problems, the better she'll understand her own, as for most people, the path to addiction is very similar.

As already mentioned, progress won't be a steady linear process. Sarah will experience bumps on the way, and sometimes she'll feel like a failure, but she mustn't let these setbacks deter her. She needs to remember that the next stage in the cycle of change is the *relapse stage*, which is when the problem you have been fighting against fights back.

Relapse is an integral part of any process involving this kind of transformation, and it happens due to the forces always working against it. If you're trying to give up smoking, you have to resist the temptation to have just one cigarette. The temptation to have only one more drink will also appear when you're trying to give up alcohol, and the people you're trying to distance yourself from will keep coming back. In a moment of weakness, you might give in.

Sarah can, therefore, expect to fall down a few times, but she must then simply dust herself down each time, and carry on. She should remember that to experience relapse having progressed through 5 stages of change is to have made progress overall. Each drawback must be treated as a blip on the way to success.

Sarah's manifesto

It's hard to stick at something for long without getting distracted. This is true of the best of us, and Sarah is likely to face this obstacle too. Staying focused requires a lot of effort, but we can make our lives easier by having a mechanism to get us back on track when we stray off-course. A written life plan, a mission statement or a personal manifesto can provide such a mechanism.

This kind of plan is a document that states your aims, ambitions and goals, and specifies how you intend to achieve them. It should indicate where you want to be in six months from now, in a year, 5 years, 10 years and even 20 years, depending on how far ahead you can envisage.

A really comprehensive life plan also outlines the resources required to achieve the set goals as well as the obstacles you're likely to come across. A document of this nature can become a guide you can refer to periodically to enable you to stay on track.

Sarah needs such a life plan, and she may write one herself or enlist the help of a mentor or life coach. She then needs to read and re-read her life plan or manifesto at regular intervals, and update it whenever she learns something new about herself or her circumstances. The lessons she's learned from her mistakes must all be included. She should never go more than a month without reading it—this will help her to avoid making the same mistakes over and over again. Sarah's manifesto could look something like this:

I Sarah would like to be known as a caring mother, a loving wife, a competent nurse and a faithful friend. My goal is to end this criminal lifestyle and start a new journey towards the fulfilment of my dreams. I know it won't be easy, and there'll be ups and downs, but I'm determined to reach my goal.

I'm going to need help, but I'm determined to do it. I intend to join a group and start forming new relationships. I'll also learn what it takes to sustain them.

I shall enrol in a college and allow the environment to shape my views and behaviour. I'll study hard for my exams, and complete all my tasks. When I leave college, I want to go to university to study nursing. My journey begins now!

Six months from now, if I am still in prison, I hope to have made strides forward in tackling my cocaine addiction, and I shall enlist the help of the Drug and Alcohol team to help me achieve this goal. I'll learn all I can about my addiction to increase my chances of overcoming it.

I also want to make use of the facilities in prison to improve myself. I shall enrol in the educational programme and use my interactions with others to shape my behaviour. I'll look for positive influences and stay away from negative ones.

I am also going to be a prolific reader. I plan to read books about personal development, and try to understand myself better. From today onward, my mistakes will become a platform for new learning.

A year from now I want to look back and say that I am no longer interested in taking cocaine or any other street drug. Five years from now I would like to have finished college. In ten years, I would like to have found a job as a nurse and started a family. I know that my plan is ambitious, but if I put my mind to it, I'll succeed.

Self-appraisal test

This might be a good time for a self-appraisal. Consider how you've lived your life. Think about the things you've prioritised and expended your time and resources on. Compare your achievements with the effort you put in and ask yourself if it was worthwhile. Look back on some of the goals you've previously pursued, and ask yourself if you followed them through to the end. If so, was it worth it?

Consider your dreams—how many of them have shaped your life? Have you abandoned them? Were those dreams valid or worth pursuing?

Consider the following domains in your life: spirituality (your relationship with God, the meaning of life, your attitude to an afterlife), connectivity (your relationship with family members and people outside of your home), health (mental and physical), personal learning and development, vocational (work and career), avocational (recreation), and lastly, aspirational (dreams and desires). Now ponder the questions below and consider how they relate to each domain. When you've completed your appraisal, draw up a life plan stating your objectives and how you're going to achieve them. Revisit that plan regularly and repeat the self-appraisal test a couple of times each year to check if you're heading in the right direction or have strayed off course.

Where am I?

- What kind of person have I become? What impression do I give when I interact with others? What do others tell me about yourself?
- What is my purpose? What have I been living for? What have I given my time and attention to? What am I passionate about?
- How do I see myself? Do I know my place in the world? Am I happy with the way people treat me, or am I often upset about how I'm treated?

- Do I feel that I deserve better? Do I speak up for myself or do I just accept unfair treatment and ignore how it made me feel? Do I overreact when people mistreat me? Am I cocky or arrogant, and is this a mask for something else?
- How do I relate to people? Do I trust them? Do I allow them to get to know me, or do I keep them at arms' length? Do I treat people fairly? How important is fairness to me?
- Am I transparent? Am I truthful? How important is truth to me? How often do I bend the facts to suit me?
- Do I lose my temper easily? When am I most likely to lose my temper? What role has my temperament played in my decisions?
- How steadfast am I in my decisions? Do I waver, or do I stand by what I've said if I'm convinced it's the truth? Am I easily swayed by my feelings and emotions when I'm trying to take a decision? Do my actions reflect my intentions? Do I sometimes sabotage my own plans?
- Do I give up easily or do I follow things through to the end? Do I get on and do things or do I procrastinate? Am I sometimes too quick to act, without having carefully looked at the facts? Do I often regret my actions?
- What character traits do I wish to possess?
- Am I operating at my full potential? If not, what are the reasons for my underachievement? Am I too afraid to take any chances? Do I have the necessary knowledge, skills, temperament, self-belief and values to achieve my dreams?

How did I get here?

- What mistakes have I made? Were there any warning signs? Did I ignore them?
- What factors have been responsible for the major decisions in my life? Think of your career choice, employment decisions, the subjects you studied in school and university, the extracurricular activities you pursued, and your relationship decisions. Then ask yourself these questions:

- How did I make those decisions? Did I allow myself enough time or did I make them too quickly? Did I obtain enough information before making those decisions? Did I let my emotions and sentiments get in the way? Do the choices I've made reflect my desires or have I been swayed by others or by my circumstances? If so, why did that happen? Did I think that other people's opinions were more important than mine? Do I give more weight to the views of others than to your own? Have I sometimes been too scared to say no? Have I made decisions as a result of being put on the spot? Are my habits hindering my progress?
- What opportunities have I missed? How did I miss them? Again, think about the following possible reasons: not having the right information, my lack of self-belief, temperament etc.
- How can I explain my failures? Consider the following points: not knowing all the facts, fear, lack of application, lack of goals, lack of self-discipline, and poor self-control.

Where do I want to be?

- What are my dreams and aspirations?
- Where would do I like to be in five, ten, and 20 years from now?
- Assuming that I live till I'm 80, how do I want to spend the rest of my life?
- What legacy would I like to leave behind? What would I like to be remembered for?

How do I get there?

- What steps do I need to take to achieve my goals?
- Do I understand what each step involves?
- Can I picture where I'm going?
- Have I come to terms with the deficits in my character, as well as in my skills and in my attitude? Do I know how to transform my character and attitude, and to develop my skills?

- Do I understand the cost of change?
- Do I know what the consequences are likely to be if I fail to effect change?
- Am I willing to do what it takes to get where I want to be?

Chapter 3

How we all get ourselves into a jam

Looking at Sarah's life, it isn't hard to see why she might want a change. She has made a hash of her life so far, and we can blame her predicament on the choices that she and her mother have made, the environment, perhaps, serving as a catalyst. But how do we explain Andy's crisis? He doesn't appear to have made any of the critical errors that Sarah has, and the environment seems to have been favourable.

Andy has a good job, a handsome salary and a happy family. Some would say his life has been perfect. In many respects, he has the things that Sarah wants. So why does he want to make a change? To understand this, we need to go back to his childhood.

As we've explained already, Andy's parents were highly driven and planned every aspect of his life, particularly his education. They started steering him towards the sciences from an early age; sure he'd do well in them. Andy was given two straight choices of study: medicine or engineering, and he chose to be an engineer. Although this was nearer to his interests than medicine, it wasn't really what he desired.

From the moment he learnt to ride a horse, Andy has wanted to be a jockey, and many people have in fact complimented him on his exceptional horsemanship. But Andy's parents didn't see this as a fitting career for their son. And as their arguments for him pursuing a career in engineering seemed more sensible than anything he could come up with, he went along with their suggestion. But he has often wondered how his life might be had he pursued his dreams.

Andy's situation isn't unique. Many are stranded in careers they didn't choose, marriages they didn't plan to be in, and alas, some are living far from the goals they'd once aspired towards. For a while, life for these people may have seemed to be going well. There was work to go to, bills to pay, and children to look after. Life kept them reasonably busy and even provided opportunities for thrills, which took their attention away from the questions they should have been asking.

But now, in the second half of their lives, the sources of adrenalin have dried up for Andy and others like him, and the question of unfulfilled dreams has raised its head. Andy wishes he could turn back the clock and pursue the career he once aspired to, but it seems too late to pursue a career in horse riding now.

The pursuit of meaning

But, does it really matter that Andy has failed to pursue his dream? Why can't he brush aside his niggling feelings, sit back and enjoy his achievements? Why not, as Gemma has suggested, find a new interest to keep him going? This is what many do when they arrive in midlife and discover they haven't fulfilled their life goals—they scramble after new goals instead or find something else to occupy themselves with. Andy could go down this route, but he knows he'd merely be prolonging his agony.

Besides, he has already gone down that path in a sense. For years he ignored his desires while he worked hard, first to meet his parents' expectations and later, to provide for his family; and there's nothing wrong with that, of course. Although these things kept him occupied and gave him a sense of purpose, now, many years later, he's still pondering his lifelong dreams. He could turn his attention to something else to keep him going, but he knows that his abandoned dreams will come back to haunt him again. That's because we all need our lives to make sense. And when the things that currently hold our attention have lost their attraction, we find ourselves gravitating back to the age-old question of meaning. Let me illustrate this with a story.

Back in the day when there were few machines around, and most jobs were done manually, a man went to a building site to look for work and was told to dig a hole. He wasn't told what the hole was for, just how much he'd earn. And since he was strapped for cash and the pay was good, he took the job.

As winter drew near, and the ground hardened, the work got more difficult, but he kept going—he had bills to pay. However, his enthusiasm for the job soon began to wane, and getting up in the morning became more of a chore.

One day, the man decided he'd had enough. He'd approach his boss and hand in his resignation. On the way to work that day, he met the architect of the project. In conversation, he learnt that the hole he'd been digging was to make room for one of the vital supporting structures of the building and that without it, the project would not succeed.

Suddenly, he realised how important his role was. Until then he hadn't felt part of the team, and his part in the project had seemed insignificant. On arrival at work that day, everyone saw a change of attitude, he seemed to have a new spring in his step, and he went home at the end of the day singing.

When his wife noticed his cheerful attitude, she thought he'd perhaps been given a raise. Only a couple of days earlier, he'd been talking about the futility of his life and had been ready to quit the job. Whatever could have happened to him? She asked herself. Has he won the lottery? When she asked him the reason for his newfound optimism, she was surprised to learn that it had nothing to do with either of her guesses.

As we can see, this man accepted the job on the basis that it would help pay his bills. For a while, this seemed a good enough reason to get up in the morning, brave the weather, and endure a hard day's work. But he soon needed more than that to motivate him, and so discovering the importance of his role gave him the boost he needed.

Money is a big motivator, and for a while, the quest to pay our bills or have a better life may provide the motivation to get through each day. But a time will come in the continuous pursuit of even the most lucrative pay when everything will become monotonous and pointless, especially if the pressure on that paycheque has eased. This is true of other motivators too—they'll all run their course. When the bills have all been paid, and the luxury goods purchased, we'll be left wondering whether there's something more. And unless we can address the question of meaning, we'll struggle with motivation.

This is why Andy is sensing the need for change. The things that once gave him a sense of purpose have all run their course. He needs an appraisal, but his assessment must go deeper than Sarah's. He needs to thoroughly address the question of meaning. If he doesn't, it'll only come up again later, when it may be too late to take action.

Finding true meaning

In the story about the man digging a hole, his motivation problem was solved when he discovered how his work was part of something bigger. But something like this may not prove a good motivator for long. Take a look at some of the employees of big companies such as Microsoft. Microsoft exists to solve a problem. Its products have helped to shape the way we live and work and have propelled our lives up onto a whole new level. Working for this corporation must give one a sense of being part of something big. Yet not every employee of Microsoft will feel fulfilled, and over the years, some will have left to join other corporations or even to set up their own businesses.

This is true of other large companies too. The National Health Service in the UK is the largest employer in Europe and one of the largest in the world. Since its inception, the NHS has helped transform millions of lives through the treatments it has provided and the research it has spearheaded. Although working in the NHS must give the staff a sense of purpose, even this organisation sees people leave their professions in pursuit of something else.

In some cases, professionals, like doctors, have left to pursue quite different careers. While some will have left for practical reasons such as better pay and working conditions, there are bound to be cases where people have left in pursuit of a greater sense of satisfaction or fulfilment. Simply being part of something big might not always satisfy our desire for meaning. We must dig deeper.

Nature has the clues

When you see squirrels gathering acorns for winter, wildebeests migrating across the plains of East Africa in search of greener pastures, or a female bear going into hibernation only to re-emerge several months later with her cubs, you get a sense of how nature exists in perfect harmony. Every creature seems to know its place in the world, *what* it's supposed to do and *when*. You don't see animals walking around looking baffled, wondering what the meaning of life is or what their next steps in life should be. And that's because they live according to their natural instincts. Each species is designed to live in a specific manner. The question of meaning is, for them, hardly relevant.

This question takes on new significance when you have more than one option because that raises the possibility that at least one of those options will not bring any sense of fulfilment. And this is the case with humans. With an intellect superior to that of animals, the possibilities open to us are seemingly endless as we can live any kind of life we like. But whatever direction we take, we risk straying far from the thing we crave the most: meaning. We can get muddled in our choices and end up living the kind of life we never wanted in the first place. We can also go after multiple pursuits only to discover much later, as the biblical character Solomon once did, that we've been chasing the wind.

Solomon was the third king of Israel and regarded, in his day, as the richest and wisest man on earth. He was very knowledgeable and was, the equivalent of a poet and natural philosopher. With riches, power and a keen intellect, Solomon set out to 'explore'. He studied every subject he could think of and pursued his every desire. "I tested myself with mirth to see if it would lead somewhere," he once said.

Solomon liked the finer things in life and sent out expeditions in search of luxurious and exotic goods from faraway lands. He built palaces adorned with gold that became the envy of neighbouring kingdoms and became one of the wonders of the world. Solomon lived "the life," if you like. But in the end, he declared: "Meaningless! Meaningless! Utterly meaningless! Everything is meaningless."

He wasn't referring to a lack of rationality in his life when he made this statement; instead, he was bemoaning the fact that none of his pursuits, however pleasurable, had brought the sense of fulfilment that he craved.

This tells us something else about *meaning*. It isn't necessarily to be found in a multiplicity of pursuits, nor in life's many delights. Instead, our pursuits need to resonate with the deeper yearnings of our souls to have any chance of yielding a sense of fulfilment.

Meaning versus purpose

In a study on the meaning of life, Canadian psychologists analysed some notable quotes from a group of famous people, The quotes from these participants correspond to the 8 major themes shown below. The percentage reflects the number of quotes that match each theme.

- Life is primarily to be enjoyed and experienced (17%)
- We live to express compassion to others, to love, to serve (13%)
- Life is unknowable, a mystery (13%)
- Life has no meaning (11%)
- We are to worship God and prepare for the afterlife (11%)
- Life is a struggle (8%)
- We are to create our own meaning in life (5%)
- Life is a joke (4%)

If the above quotes accurately represent the views of the study participants, then the majority believe that life has no meaning as such, and we're at liberty to attach to it our own personal meaning. Alternatively, we can forget about meaning altogether and just enjoy it as best we can.

I've yet to come across a similar study on the general population, but it wouldn't surprise me if it yielded similar results. The truth is that most people don't believe that life has any meaning, and many would suggest that we should simply enjoy the journey. And I can see the appeal in that approach. It's doubtless better to live happily with no sense of purpose than to be miserable while wondering about the meaning of life. Equally, it's more profitable to assign to your life any meaning you want than to live without one. But I'd like to suggest something better than both these approaches: *living for your purpose*. Let me illustrate this with another story:

A man overslept on a train and ended up in a small town in the middle of nowhere. Attempts to get back on another train and head for his original destination failed, so he ended up staying. Fortunately, someone took him in and was extremely kind to him, so after a few more failed attempts to leave the town, he decided to make that place his home. He found himself a job, one thing led to another, and now, several months later, he's running for the position of head of the town planning committee. Whether he's elected or not, we can all agree that he's done remarkably well. He's managed to turn a desperate situation into a success, having found something meaningful to do with his life while "lost." Here's the backstory.

This man had a family and was on his way to the next town where he was supposed to pick up medication for his little daughter, who was seriously ill. While asleep on the train he suffered a mini-stroke, which caused him to lose his memory. This is why he was unable to find his way back. His daughter has since died, unfortunately, as a consequence of him failing to return with the medication. His family, and indeed the whole town are in distress, not only because of the daughter's death, but also because they are missing their newly elected mayor. Search parties have been sent out but to no avail. Everyone is left in limbo, unsure whether to mourn his death or hope for his arrival.

Now that you know a lot more about the story, I expect you'll feel differently about his achievements. When we consider the distress of his family and of the entire community, we cannot help but think that his accomplishments don't mean very much after all. We must all now just want him to return home. Once he recovers his memory, the man himself will be desperate to be reunited with his family.

Can you now see the difference between living for your purpose and finding something meaningful to do? This man was pursuing a definite purpose before the stroke forced him to change course. He was then left to make the most of what could have been a hopeless situation, and he managed to do it very well. If we consider his life within the narrow context of that town and his time there, he's practically a hero, but when you can see beyond his immediate circumstances, it's clear that he was actually in a very difficult situation.

Likewise with ourselves; there's a reason for us being here—we have a purpose that should be directing our lives. We can give meaning to our lives by doing something useful. That is better than sitting around wondering why we're here. But we can also reach inside and discover our purpose, and if we do, we'll unlock our full potential.

Purpose brings true meaning

If someone gave you a gift, and you didn't know what it was for, you wouldn't be able to utilise it as the manufacturer intended, but you might still find some use for it. If it looked decorative, you could display it somewhere in your house, or alternatively, it might be something your children could play with. In both cases, you'd have given the item a purpose. But you'd also know that the item wasn't necessarily being used as intended and you'd be pleased when you found the user manual. Reading it, you'd probably discover that what the manufacturer had in mind was far superior to the use you'd given it.

It's the same in life. You can give your life meaning by doing something useful, but that may not be what you were really meant to do, and in comparison with your true purpose, you might be underachieving. You can only realise your potential and attain the heights you were destined to reach if you discover your purpose.

Don't ignore the calls of your soul!

When asked about the purpose of life, many suggest that it's to be happy. But can this really explain our existence and our behaviour? Why, for example, do some people abandon their families and embark on expeditions to remote parts of the world? Why do some tread treacherous paths and endure extreme weather conditions to get to the top of the highest mountains or the ends of the earth? Why do scientists spend thousands of hours in a laboratory, inventing things they'll never profit from? How do we account for man's need to continually improve himself, do things better, reach the moon, explore space? All these questions we'll struggle to answer if we believe that the purpose of life is simply to be happy.

Could a quest for happiness alone drive people towards such sacrifices? Did Sir Edmund Hilary and others endure much pain to get to the top of Mt. Everest in pursuit of happiness? Was Bill Gates after happiness when he abandoned his first-class education at Harvard University in search of the software that could power home computers? Perhaps some vague link exists between these men's actions and a desire to be happy, but this alone cannot explain their behaviour.

Something else must have been driving them to make those decisions, and I dare say that it wasn't a desire to live a meaningful life either, as good as that may sound. Living a meaningful life doesn't require any extraordinary steps—all it takes is to work hard, raise a family and engage in a few acts of kindness here and there. These things can give one a sense of living a meaningful life. So why do some people need to go to extremes such as abandoning their education or departing on a journey from which they may not return? Why do some people go against the expectations of everyone around them to achieve their personal ambition instead? It seems it's destiny.

There's a call from within their souls they can't ignore, and their actions are a response to this cry. We often sense it in the latter half of our lives. As the hustle and bustle dies down, the groaning from within gets louder as it were and some of us get restless. But not everyone senses this or those who do, don't understand it. Some treat it as a natural phase of life, a storm to be weathered, but others go and see their doctors and are prescribed anti-depressants. If your soul is crying out to you; how long will you ignore it for?

> *The purpose of life is not to be happy. It is to be useful, to be honourable, to be compassionate, and to have it make some difference that you have lived and lived well.*

> Ralph Waldo Emerson

We've all been wired in such a way as to have natural passions, appetites and drives. These are the body's warning systems and motivators. When the tummy rumbles, we know it's time to replenish our energies, and we respond by having a meal. When we feel an urge to use the bathroom, we know it means we need to empty our bladders so that the body may rid itself of unwanted substances. Likewise, when our eyes begin to shut despite our best efforts to stay awake, we know it's time to go to bed to renew our strength. But did you know that a similar principle applies to the soul? The soul issues signals about certain things we need to do in our lives, although many of us are oblivious of these signals. Just as you cannot ignore the urge to use the bathroom, you cannot ignore the calls of your soul indefinitely without suffering the consequences. As the body shouts out for food, so, the soul cries out for a purpose.

We've all been created for a purpose, and that purpose isn't happiness. You can attempt living for pleasure, but you'll run out of steam sooner or later. You can focus your energies on the quest for survival, but you'll lose your sense of purpose after you've paid your bills. You may choose to build your life around your family, but a time will come when you'll feel less needed, and when this happens, you'll experience emptiness and abandonment.

This is what happened to Andy. While his children were younger, they gave meaning to his endeavours. Purchasing presents and watching the excitement on their faces as they tore through the packaging to get to the toys kept him going. But now life has slowed down, and the bills are all taken care of. The children now choose their own presents and purchase them online. The things that kept Andy going are no more, and he is back facing the questions he should have been asking himself a long while ago. The answer to those questions is the ultimate motivator: purpose.

Purpose drives out chaos

When you have a goal, mental weariness disappears. Boredom and confusion no longer plague you, having no place in a purpose-driven life. Having a purpose brings stability and certainty, and it ends the constant drifting and vacillating. The reason you keep moving from one thing to another and are unable to complete your projects is due to a lack of purpose. You cannot answer the question, *Why*. The day you discover the answer, you'll stop vacillating and start to live much more intensely. You'll also learn to persevere to the end. To prove this to you, please allow me to tell you something about myself. I started writing a book in 2007 and still haven't finished it. I started another 2 years later and haven't managed to publish it either. I started this book 3 months ago, and it's going to be ready for editing this month. The difference is that I found a purpose! Previously I wrote because I enjoyed it, but since I discovered my purpose, everything has changed. Now it's a race to get my books published.

Purpose harnesses your resources

Every natural resource we possess—our bodies, minds, and talents have all been designed to serve our purpose, and will only be put to full and proper use when we find it. The soul comes into its own when we're treading the paths of destiny, and it makes its hidden resources available to us. The desire to succeed, and the tenaciousness and willingness to persevere, in spite of all the challenges, spring forth from within and drive us forward when we are pursuing our purpose. Fear departs from our hearts because our focus is no longer on ourselves but on our goals. Having a purpose gives us belief and removes the constant doubting that often accompanies merely doing "something meaningful". When you have a purpose, you'll refuse to take "no" for an answer. Nothing will deter you. This is why you need to discover your purpose.

Key facts:

- There 's a reason for our existence
- Having a purpose brings meaning to our lives
- Living a meaningful life does not equate to living for your purpose
- Treading the path of destiny beats finding something useful to do
- Your calling will energise you and give you focus
- Purpose drives out chaos

- Your purpose is your answer to the question of *Why*
- Lack of purpose often leads to despair
- Your purpose will bring out your potential

Some points to consider:

- What is your purpose?
- Are you living for your purpose?
- Does your life make sense to you?
- Do you feel fulfilled?
- Where are you heading in life?
- Are you operating below your potential?

Go to a quiet place and carefully consider these questions. Think until you come up with some answers.

Chapter 4

Abandoned dreams

Having a purpose keeps us focused, as we've already established. But did you know that without the ability to dream, we may not complete the assignment for which we have been sent to earth? This is because our dreams are pictorial representations of our purpose. When we dream, we're catapulted into the future, and since our mission is in the future, we're able to catch glimpses of it.

When my children were younger, I often watched cartoon movies with them. One of my favourites was Meet the Robinsons. This movie is about a boy called Lewis, who lives in a children's home. He doesn't know his birth parents and desires to be loved. Being a bit of a geek, Lewis likes making things, which he then shows off to prospective adoptive parents in the hope of being chosen. But each time something goes wrong. The children's home gradually empties as the children are taken for adoption; but Lewis and his roommate Goob aren't so lucky.

One day, Lewis makes a memory scanner. He hopes it will help him retrieve memories of his mother who abandoned him as a child. He also wants to show off his invention at a science fair in the hope of impressing a couple who've shown an interest in adopting him. Unfortunately for Lewis, someone tampers with the device while he's asleep, and it malfunctions. The science fair then ends in disaster, which scares the couple away, and they decide not to adopt Lewis after all. Cruel, I should say, but then this is only a movie. Lewis is understandably upset and decides not to make any more inventions.

At this point, a boy named Wilbur arrives from the future. He takes Lewis to his future where he sees himself married and living a happy life.

Lewis discovers that his future self is a great inventor, and that's because he didn't give up inventing things after the "disaster" at the science fair. Wilbur takes Lewis back in time and tells him not to give up his passion; otherwise, the future life Lewis saw will not materialise.

This movie depicts the way that dreams can operate. In this case, they're a vision of what the future holds, but this vision isn't guaranteed to happen. It depends on whether we put in the effort to realise it. By travelling forward in time, Lewis could see the kind of life he could achieve if he'd commit himself to creating it. It would mean enduring disappointments, failures and frustrations. He'd also need to avoid distractions and stop himself from being side-tracked. Only then would he fulfil his dreams. But as we shall soon see, this outcome is easier to achieve in a cartoon than it usually is in real life.

Why we abandon our dreams

If you ask a group of children what they want to do when they grow up, many will tell you without any hesitation. When a teacher asked her class this question, some of the children said they wanted to be firemen, and others wanted to be doctors, teachers, police officers or nurses. One wanted to be a car, showing the wider range of a child's imagination.

Children understand that their lives are supposed to count for something, and their aspirations reflect this. Those childhood dreams may be a little off and lack substance, but they usually become more realistic as children grow up. The child who wanted to be a car probably has a desire to move at high speed, so his dream may well turn into an ambition to be a Formula One racing driver. But consistency in holding onto one specific dream is unusual as most children abandon those early dreams by the time they're adults.

Occasionally, one may come across a young man or woman, perhaps a university student, who has grand ambitions and dreams. Some will talk about their desire to be world leaders or lead a campaign and make a difference in their world. It's always heartening to know that such people still exist, although an encounter with the same person a few years later may prove a very different experience. If they've landed a job and are managing to pay their bills, then one may still detect in them traces of their dreams, but those that are jobless will often be despondent. Their only goal now may be to simply find a job, start earning a living and end their dependency on parents. The prospect of achieving their ambitions will at this point seem very distant.

In the case of an enthusiastic student who has abandoned their dreams, the obvious cause is an unpleasant collision with life as an adult. The challenge of finding a job in an economy where even the most experienced often remain unemployed can be blamed. But the phenomenon of abandoned dreams is far too common an occurrence to blame on a single cause. The truth is, that whether you're struggling to find a job after school or have already secured one and you appear to be doing well, you've probably said goodbye to your dreams. It seems that life is designed in such a way as to rid you of your dreams at the earliest opportunity.

Love is in the air

Marriage is one example of an experience that sometimes leaves people feeling disillusioned, and can shatter their dreams. It's often the reason for the loss of many dreams, and yet this truth is often forgotten by those making preparations for the great day. People get carried away with excitement and start dreaming about the future with their loved ones, but often, they haven't fully realised how their shared life will be very different from the future they'd planned before they met each other. That might be okay; marriage does involve compromises after all. But I've also seen how some individuals planning their lives together often dream about quite different futures. One may be wishing to continue on the same trajectory as before, while the other may be hoping for a radical change.

It is said that men want their wives to remain as they were when they met them, whereas women want to change their husbands into the persons they want them to be. This may be a rather over-simplistic view of marriage, but it does highlight the fact that people often want different things from life. Thus, two people planning their lives together may, in the secrecy of their hearts, be imagining two very different futures. But in the heady days leading up to the wedding, they blind themselves to these differences.

The critical moment arrives when the initial warmth and optimism start to fade. Suddenly, they realise that they haven't been living their dreams, neither those they'd had before meeting their spouse, nor the ones that were conjured up in the heat of romance. No wonder many marriages suffer a crisis at this point.

You see, dreams are not merely a product of fantasy; they're how your soul carves out an image of the future for you. When, as a child, you imagined yourself as a dancer, an artist or an aeronautical engineer, you weren't merely fantasising; but were actually trying to paint a picture of the future. You were then supposed to go on and create it. That image, vague at its inception, was supposed to develop into an elaborate plan upon which to build your life. Falling in love with someone doesn't change that. Your soul still wants to do those things you once dreamt about. Without being aware of it though, you might mortgage your future by tying it to a relationship before you've had a chance to see how your dreams can be turned into reality.

Imagine yourself on a walk in the countryside, and spotting a beautiful castle in the distance. Your dream is that castle. You may not know how to get to it, but as long as you keep it in view, you stand a chance of reaching it eventually. Taking your eyes off it would make reaching it much harder. While you're making your way towards the castle, a stranger comes along asking for directions, and you, wanting to be helpful, jump in their car to help them get to their destination.

Will your actions take you closer to your destination? Possibly, the ride could bring you closer to the castle, but equally, it could take you further away. If you lose sight of the castle, the chances are you'll never get to it. This is what we do with our dreams; we jump into relationships before we know how to achieve them. And some of us get into the car without having the faintest idea about the kind of future we want. We may simply hope that marriage itself will provide the answers to life's most important questions.

Then, failing to stay alert once we're in the car, we find secondary goals for our lives and forget about those important questions. We get drawn into a quest for daily survival and amble down life's many corridors that lead nowhere until life slows down. Then the dreams we were once pursuing resurface.

Are you beginning to see your mistakes? Perhaps you're starting to feel anguish. If so, don't fret; there's a lot of good news on the way. Hold back from taking any drastic decisions because the moment of heightened emotions is not the time to make any decisions, let alone important ones. Just let the realisation of what you've done sink in. Take time out to ponder your life. Book a lone holiday somewhere and think, think, think. But most importantly, keep reading.

Fatal realism

Another critical moment for dreams is when children appear on the scene. Children are a bundle of joy as we all know. They put a smile on our faces, rejuvenate us and give us a reason to keep going. But the truth is that the moment of their arrival is also the moment when many dreams are abandoned.

Take a young couple that has just had a baby, for instance. For argument's sake let's say that the pregnancy wasn't planned. Chances are they'll have to put their plans on hold as they make preparations for the new arrival, and it's right to do that. But without a considerable effort to get back on track, the dreams will be shelved for good.

A young couple with an ambition of owning a business may, for instance, choose to work part-time while they devote time to achieving their dream, but with the arrival of a child, one of them, or possibly even both, will end up working full-time to earn the extra money needed for the upkeep of the family. This will often mean less time for the project, and if they go on to have more children, their business will never materialise. This may sound like a rather pessimistic view of the family, but the point we're trying to make is that life is full of such responsibilities and distractions that take us on a detour away from our dreams. If you don't live mindfully, then you're bound to just accept them.

And when it comes to adapting to the new situation, women beat men hands down. I once heard a man describe how easily his wife adjusted after their first baby was born. "My wife and I were both dreamers when we first met, but I was shocked to see how quickly she became a 'realist' after our first child arrived, he said. I was still a dreamer, pretty much, but she was gone. Talking to her was like talking to a different person. She was just looking at the reality of our situation and planning our lives according to how she saw it".

Many would agree with this man's observation that women are quicker off the mark when it comes to the parenting role. The woman is often the more practical partner in the relationship, and her attention to detail helps to cover all the bases. Some of this comes down to maternal instinct and societal expectations of the role of women.

But I've also discovered that this ability to adapt easily doesn't always serve women well. Sometimes they adjust to the point of losing touch with their dreams, and they often expect their spouses to do the same. This may then cause tension because the "less practical" partner may experience this adaptation as their dreams being crushed.

The harsh realities of life

Those of you who know the story of Joseph, a popular West End theatre show, but also a story in the Bible, know that disclosing his dreams was Joseph's undoing. In one dream, Joseph had seen the sun, the moon and twelve stars bow down to him. As soon as his father heard of this, he was alarmed because in those days people took dreams seriously. Was he, his wife and his twelve other children about to bow down to Joseph? He wondered.

As for Joseph's brothers, they were so unhappy with his dreams as to contemplate killing him. In the end, they sold him to a group of merchants travelling to Egypt.

Following a few challenges, Joseph found his life in Egypt turned in his favour. He'd go on to become the second most powerful man in the country. His family later joined him in Egypt, where he ruled over them just as he'd seen in his dreams.

The moral of this story is that the world may not applaud your dreams. As a matter of fact, your aspirations might cause concern because they're likely to be far removed from the reality on the ground. And some people might deem it necessary to give you a "reality check" as they call it, although, a more appropriate term would be: "putting a damper on your dreams". What they fail to understand is that dreams are supposed to be wild, and sometimes totally unrealistic because they're a vision of the future. The more distant that future is, the more bizarre the dream will seem.

How would you have reacted, for example, if you'd been around when Bill Gates voiced his vision of a computer in every home? Would you have thought that his dream was realistic? Remember that this was in the 70s when most people didn't know what a computer looked like, and the average business still couldn't afford one. His was a wild dream, and yet it's now a reality in nearly every part of the world. We can't help but be grateful that Bill Gates didn't abandon his vision, as the world today might be a very different place otherwise. He didn't, and neither must you, no matter how unrealistic your dream may seem.

Premature action

Sometimes people who tell us to abandon our dreams do so out of concern for our welfare. Some of them have tried pursuing theirs and failed, others were shoved down one of life's many corridors littered with ready-made career templates, and told about the dangers of following your heart. These people chose to conform, and have developed a fear of what's out there by doing so. They cannot imagine living their dreams, and the thought of someone else doing so absolutely terrifies them, especially if that someone is a loved one who doesn't have a swelling bank account to back them up. Therefore, they offer their advice to spare you the agony of failure, but their "act of kindness" comes from the perspective of someone who hasn't dared to live.

Many young people with dreams, understanding the reason for this kind of advice, decide to ignore the cautions of loved ones as they shoot off in pursuit of their destiny. Often, they still have no idea of how to achieve their dreams, but sensing a threat to their ambitions, they go off anyway, only to return home later battered and bruised, and probably to hear the words "I told you so" echo in their ears. And so they take their place among many of life's dream casualties. From that time onwards, the idea of going after your dreams will seem silly. If only they knew that dreams take time to mature, and that a threat to your dreams shouldn't trigger such premature action.

Living by instinct

We mentioned earlier, the perfectly attuned lives of animals, where the question of meaning is practically redundant. Living according to instinct requires little planning. Certain creatures do plan ahead to some degree, however. Ants from the subfamily of Myrmicinae, for example, grow fungus for food, and this involves careful planning. The hunting activity of predators requires some planning too. But by and large, animals live by instinct. They rely on their natural urges and impulses and the cues that nature provides. In winter, storks fly off to Africa, and bears go into hibernation; then that pattern is reversed when spring arrives.

The lives of animals are much simpler than ours. Their food doesn't need any cooking, and their homes can be built from materials that nature provides in abundance. They don't have to go to school and have no desire to pursue a career or get rich. They leave no legacy behind either, and when they're gone, as far as we can tell, they're gone.

But our life is more complex, and cannot be lived by instinct or on autopilot. We can't afford to be passive or expect to be handed on a silver platter the information we need for our development. We must go out and actively study our environments to uncover the bountiful opportunities, as well as the dangers to avoid. We need to plan carefully, making use of every piece of information we can lay our hands on. Only then can we be guaranteed to make the most of our lives.

And yet like the animals, we too live by instinct. We fail to plan our lives or study our environment, just expecting everything to fall into place. We meet someone whose beauty or charm strikes us so much that we drastically change our plans. We go against logic, conventional wisdom and research findings and act as our feelings dictate. But worst of all, we fail to ask questions.

The best way to get to any destination if you don't have a map or a satnav is to ask for directions. Ideally, you should ask two or three people, and compare their answers. If the answers are consistent, then you know you're on the right track. If you choose not to ask anyone, you might lose your way. Equally, asking only one person may lead you further astray because they might give you the wrong directions.

The same applies in life; we cannot make much progress without seeking guidance. Guidance will come from our families, friends, mentors, coaches and teachers. It also comes from the random people we come into contact with every day, as well as from books. We also need to ask questions because not all knowledge can be taught, some of it should be actively sought. We need to take control of our lives and ask questions so that we may find our way. For some reason, children are best at doing this.

Children start asking questions the moment they learn to say "why", and they keep on asking questions, sometimes, without knowing the reason. Sadly, we lose this habit as we grow older. This may be due to our experiences. We may have been made to look stupid for asking a question at some point. But many of us have stopped asking questions because we think we've figured things out.

Teenagers stop seeking answers from their parents because they want to figure things out themselves, and in a sense, this is a good thing; it's essential that they learn to stand on their own feet. But often they stop seeking answers from their parents because they no longer consider them as an authority.

As children grow older, they look to their teachers and peers to teach them what they don't know. But they only spend a few hours a day with their teachers, and opportunities for asking questions are limited; hence their peers end up being their primary source of information. But their peers are just as clueless about life as they are. Therefore, children arrive in adulthood without answers to some of life's most important questions. It's hardly surprising that their lives should descend down one of life's many blind alleys. And they won't realise it until much later when their dreams may seem unachievable.

A quest for survival

Life for many of us has become a constant pursuit of the next paycheque, and very often it isn't enough to see us through to the next cheque. The task of survival is often so intense that there's hardly any time to think beyond maintaining our existence, and the cyclical nature of this struggle makes it impossible to notice anything beyond that cycle.

We get up in the morning, get the children ready for school, go to work, come back, prepare dinner, go to bed and do the same thing again the next day. And for some, weekends bring no respite, we shoot off to our second or even third jobs or drive the children to their activities. Everywhere you look you see this intense struggle, people going round and round in circles doing the same things week in, week out. Everyone wishes that life could be different, but no one knows how to get off this hamster wheel of life. The tempo is fast, and the potential for disaster is ever-present. One false move, and you could be drowned in debt. The only way out, it seems, is to keep going till one literally drops dead or is hit by some crisis. This, unfortunately, is the plight of the vast majority of the human race, and in this struggle for survival, following your dreams seems like a luxury only the rich can indulge in. If only we knew that our dreams are our get-out-of-jail card.

Key facts:

- Dreams are your guide to the future
- Your dreams are the pictorial representation of your purpose
- Dreams keep your purpose alive
- Premature implementation of your dreams can lead to disappointment
- Dreams get lost in our struggle to survive
- Dreams get lost during life's transitions
- Simply following your feelings and instincts means leaving your dreams to die
- Dreams are meant to be wild, so don't be afraid to have dreams that seem unrealistic

Some points to consider:

- Do you still dream?
- What's happened to your dreams?

- How did you lose them?
- Why is your life heading in the direction it is?

Go to a quiet place and take these questions with you. Consider them until you come up with some answers.

Chapter 5

Getting back on track

In the movie, *The Bridges of Madison County*, Francesca, played by Meryl Streep, meets Robert, a National Geographic photographer and has a four-day extramarital affair that changes both their lives forever. She contemplates leaving her husband and children and travelling the world with Robert but decides against it when she realises the impact it could have on them.

This movie may be fictional, but I've often wondered whether it reflects the reality of many people's lives. The question I've always asked is; why would a respectable married woman contemplate leaving her loving husband and children in pursuit of an adventure with a stranger? One day, as I was enjoying a walk in a park, the answer to that question suddenly hit me. Dreams! This was an Italian war bride who perhaps had a very different vision of the future before meeting her husband. And though she was now living what many would describe as a meaningful life, it wasn't quite what she had once imagined.

Then comes the photographer, bringing with him a scent of the future she'd once dreamt about. In a split second, she forgets she's someone's wife, and her imagination goes to work; then the possibility of living her dreams suddenly arises. It's easy to focus on the inappropriateness of her actions and miss the more important point of why she acted this way.

Dreams are a potent force capable of steering a person's life, often without the person even knowing it. These dreams, when they remain unfulfilled, become hidden landmines waiting to go off. The faintest hope of fulfilment is enough to trigger this force, which can suddenly break through to the surface with dramatic effect. If we spot that opportunity, we'll grab it with both hands before actually thinking about the mess that might result. Such is the power of dreams, and we ignore them at our own peril. But that strong force need not remain hidden, nor should its power be a source of trouble—we can bring it out into the open and harness it for good!

Why dreaming is important

There are many ways to discover your purpose in life. You can find it in your passion and interests, and you may also chance upon your life mission by harnessing your potential, but the surest way to get to your life's destination is through dreaming. Some call it visualising or imagining; I call it dreaming.

A builder translates into brick and mortar the building the architect has drawn in ink. The drawings the builder uses are the product of the architect's imagination; they are his dreams. Because of his ability to visualise, the architect can clearly imagine a building before it's built. He can see how the different spaces in the building will be used and people moving in and out of the building long before the foundation has been laid. And when he sits down to produce the drawings for his buildings, he merely reproduces what he has already seen. Such is the power of the imagination; it enables us to peer into the future and participate in its creation.

As for the builder, his work is made that much easier when he has the architect's drawings. All he needs to do is carefully follow the plans to construct the building. If any part of it is later destroyed in bad weather, he can rebuild it by referring to the drawings. And the same is true of our lives: as a builder relies on architectural drawings, so we too build our lives on our dreams. If we get stuck, we have a blueprint to refer to.

The woes of modern-day navigation

Dreaming is also our navigation system because it allows us to get to our destination with less hassle. Before satnavs, people used maps for directions. You'd look carefully at the map before setting out, and pay particular attention to road signs, landmarks and anything else that would help you remember the way back. If you were lucky to have someone with you, then you got them to act as your co-pilot. They read the map while you drove, and made sure you stayed on track. If it was your spouse, then arguments were not unknown, as many couples will testify. Satnavs have changed all that by making travel so much easier. Now couples can avoid such strife, even if they lose the way. Who knows, satnavs may have saved many marriages too.

But, for all the benefits they bring, satnavs have made us lazy. Today few of us feel any need to memorise the routes we're travelling on and should the satnav malfunction suddenly; we may get lost. It's the same in life: when you're guided by your dreams, you're like a driver without a satnav. You keep your eyes open and look out for opportunities and threats. You also ask questions and leave nothing to chance. In the process, you become proficient at navigating the paths of life.

If you've ever met someone who lost both parents as a child or suffered some hardship but went on to become successful, you'll have noticed how they seemed to have the answers to the questions you struggle with. Such people often appear more mature for their age, and that's because they've had to live without a satnav as it were. Having grown up with no one to dictate what their next steps in life should be, they've had to grow up quickly and figure things out for themselves. And they'll have done it by visualising their future. By comparison, life now as an adult seems a breeze.

Those of us that have had our lives planned for us are like the driver with a satnav. We may have achieved a measure of success, but we'll have done it by following our parents' instructions. Following our dreams now seems a daunting task. This is why Andy is feeling stuck. He's lived a successful life, but he has done it by following his parents' plan. He hasn't learned to create his own roadmaps as it were. But he needn't worry because there is a way out of his predicament. And you've guessed it: dreaming.

Re-routing

A builder's mistakes may be costly, but they're remediable. If necessary, the whole structure can be pulled down and rebuilt. This will doubtless increase the cost, not to mention the delays in project completion, but by and large, most mistakes that a builder makes can be resolved, and that's because he has a blueprint to refer to. Unfortunately, we can't do the same with our lives. We can't undo our mistakes.

Moreover, our lives are constantly changing. If nothing else, we are ageing, and with age comes changing fortunes—the plan we once had for our lives may no longer be applicable. If we had a dream of owning a business, we might find that demand for the product or service we'd planned to sell has shifted.

Also, others may have got ahead of us and set up similar businesses, thereby creating competition that might cause us to fail. That's not to say that old dreams should be discarded, but rather that we need to check that they're still realistic and adapt them if necessary.

Andy's dream of becoming a jockey may no longer be achievable, not least because of his age, but he can use it as his starting point nonetheless and create new dreams. To do so, he must re-ignite his interests and find the right conditions for his personal development. Dreams are like fire. They need to be kindled and kept going, and personal development is, among other things, what's needed to keep them going.

Andy has neglected his passion because he hasn't wanted to stir up old feelings, but to find his purpose now he needs to re-open a chapter that has remained closed for a long time. He needs to re-ignite his interest in horses and unleash his imagination. Just as an architect imagines the future and creates it, so must Andy visualise a different kind of life for himself.

The environment matters

Recently, I saw a documentary about a boy growing up on the streets of Lagos, Nigeria. It's not clear how he ended up there, but his story is unlikely to be any different from that of Africa's many other abandoned children. Gradually, he transforms himself into a hardened criminal who, together with his cohorts, would terrorise the neighbourhoods. At the tender age of 12, he was addicted to marijuana, which he was smoking regularly. If someone had asked him at that point what his dreams were, his answer would not have been a heart-warming one. He looked like he was on his way to becoming an even worse nightmare than he was already.

One day his path crosses that of a pastor of a church, who takes an interest in his plight. The pastor gets him off the streets and into school, and he also gets him to start playing tennis. He maintains a personal interest in the boy, phoning him regularly and visiting him. One day, the pastor asks what the boy wants to do when he grows up. Now that's a crucial question to ask a child. By asking that question, you're inviting the child to peer into the future and tell you what they can see; you're encouraging them to dream. This gives you the chance to shape their dreams.

The boy answers the pastor's question without any hesitation—he wants to be a pastor and a lawyer when he grows up. Note that he didn't need anyone to tell him what his aspirations should be. He already had in him a desire to make his life count. On the streets, he could only aspire to be an even worse crook than he already was, but in the right environment, his mind went to work to produce new images of the future.

If you live in a small village in a remote part of the world with no access to TV, the internet or a library, and where no one has any high aspirations, you're going to have a hard time dreaming about something big. You're going to have to change your environment to change the course of your life.

The environment plays a more significant role in shaping our lives than we think. A positive environment stirs the imagination and modulates our interests. It also provides the opportunities needed for our development. If the boy in the documentary film had remained on the streets, a very different future would have awaited. He's also unlikely to have become interested in playing tennis.

Andy is going to have to pay attention to his environment if he is to re-create his dreams. He'll need to surround himself with people who'll inspire him and be more accommodating of his desire to pursue his dreams. People generally fall into three categories regarding their response to others' aspirations. Some cheer even when they don't understand what's going on. These are the well-wishers, and they're usually in your inner circle, that is, your friends and family. Others offer words of encouragement and support because they understand what it means to follow your heart. Such people are open to experience and are often pursuing their own dreams.

The third group of people are the so-called "realists" who don't appreciate other people's aspirations unless they can see a clear path to fulfilment. Some in this group are quick to shoot down any dream they deem to be unrealistic. Andy needs to be mindful of this and shield his dreams while they're still in an embryonic form, lest someone talks him out of pursuing them.

An evolving picture

It's important to know that dreams aren't static. In the documentary, the boy wanted to be a pastor and a lawyer when he grew up, but those aspirations aren't set in stone. We mustn't forget that he's still a child, and those dreams are his first glimpses of the future. The more opportunities he's exposed to, the more he'll learn about himself. And as his interests and natural disposition manifest, he'll gain a better idea of the future he wants to create. Who knows? He might even decide to pursue a career in tennis. All it would take is continual development in this area, and meeting another role model, someone like Roger Federer or Novak Djokovic.

In Andy's case, the dream of becoming a jockey never materialised, but he needn't feel bad about failing to pursue it. By starting to dream again, he can create a new vision of the future.

Shaping up for the journey ahead

To get to where he needs to be, Andy will need to learn some new skills. So far, most of his personal development has centred on his job as is usually the case with professionals. But now, to stand any chance of fulfilling his dreams, Andy, just as anyone else in that situation, needs to widen the scope of his development.

Andy needs to return to school, but not necessarily to formal education. He should enrol in the school of life to discover the path he needs to take to fulfil his dreams. There aren't any schools out there that will teach him this skill, so he needs to find a way to learn it himself. Reading books on personal development and seeking out mentorship and coaching as appropriate will help equip him to pursue his new life.

Key facts:

- Dreams are the blueprint for our lives
- Dreams are our navigation system guiding us to our purpose
- Abandoning your dreams can lead to a crisis later in life
- Reconnecting with your dreams can lead to irrational behaviour
- Dreams need knowledge and an optimal environment to develop
- Dreams need protecting from adverse conditions

Some points to consider:

- What did you dream of doing or becoming when you were a child?
- Do you still dream? How often?
- Have you ever mocked your own dreams?
- Are you ashamed of your dreams? Do you think of them as being silly or unrealistic?
- Are your dreams still achievable or do they need adapting?

How can your dreams help you get back on track?

Chapter 6

Pursuing your dreams

So far, we've seen how abandoning your dreams can lead to problems later in life. Equally, an unplanned encounter with old abandoned aspirations can spell trouble. With this in mind, we must do everything in our power to cling on to our dreams. But how do we achieve this goal in a world where everything seems designed to take our dreams away? Answering this question will be the focus of this chapter.

Pursuing aspirational dreams

As we mentioned earlier, dreaming starts in childhood, and this is, therefore, the time when we begin to catch glimpses of our future. However, a childhood dream often lacks substance and needs time and the right conditions to develop. Ideally, this process must proceed alongside the development of our talents and interests so that by the time we're 18, we know what we want to do in our adult lives. Our career choices should then reflect our aspirations. But this is hardly ever the case, and in many instances, children arrive in adulthood clueless about what to do with their lives. There are many reasons for this situation.

Take, for instance, a child who dreams of becoming an artist. She may have shown signs of her creative edge through the eye-catching pictures she has produced from an early age. But she's likely to come across an education system that lays no emphasis on the development of her talent. She'll be taught subjects that the system believes she needs. The focus will be on Maths, Science and English (or another native language, according to where she lives); whereas the subject the child

is most gifted in will be taught only once a week for three-quarters of an hour.

As a result, she won't have many opportunities to develop her talent, and since the development of someone's natural abilities is essential in finding their purpose, this child is likely to struggle with deciding on her future career.

The men in our family are all teachers

Another obstacle a child might face is the expectations of others. Many parents expect their children to pursue careers that reflect their own personal ambitions rather than their children's. It sounds awful, but it's not as rare as you might think. Most parents want to give their children opportunities they didn't have when they were growing up, and that's admirable, but many also secretly hope that their children will attain the heights they failed to achieve themselves. And these parents end up choosing careers for their children to fulfil their own secret ambitions. The line between these two kinds of expectation is a fine one, and many cross it without realising it.

Family tradition can also play a part. In some families, the men are expected to join the army or become teachers, and a child might be under pressure to do the same.

Further obstacles can be placed by the wider society. In some countries, for example, children are expected to pursue careers that are considered prestigious such as medicine, law or engineering. This may sound too prescriptive, but before you condemn it, you should know how such an approach may be based on a lot of wisdom. These careers generally offer a good salary, and in the case of medicine, greater job security; benefits you wouldn't want to ignore if you lived in a developing country.

Besides, the developed world has its fair share of ready-made career templates that it expects children to choose from. In a nutshell, the choice of a career, for many children, has nothing to do with their natural abilities or their calling but is often a matter of meeting other people's expectations. And as children progress through careers that are

far removed from what they'd imagined, they move further and further away from their dreams.

The conveyor belt will kill you

Career pathways are like conveyor belts. You step on it at one end and come out at the other end as a professional who slots neatly into an establishment role. And as you progress through the factory, you'll be moulded into the shape required to make you more useful to society. You'll also change in ways you would never have anticipated, and your horizons may narrow to the point where you're almost incapable of thinking outside the box.

Take medical students, for example. They're not only taught how to treat illnesses but also how to fit into a hospital environment. They learn to sift through lots of information and focus on what they need to make a diagnosis.

Medical students also learn to make decisions quickly. Having mastered the skill of convergent thinking, a doctor can make decisions on the spot. But if this same skill is allowed to operate in life outside the hospital, it can be a handicap. The reason is that the paths of life don't run in straight lines, and the most direct routes aren't necessarily the best or the most rewarding. True discovery is made when we allow ourselves to be taken on a ride and go with the flow. But if we've spent vast amounts of time following a strict regime, narrowing down options and seeking the quickest route to our goals, which is often the case in medicine, then we might end up approaching life in the same way and find it a very unsatisfactory experience.

I remember how I felt when a colleague, a fellow medical practitioner, informed me that he was taking a career break to take up a hotel manager position in an exotic location. I couldn't think of a single reason why he'd want to do that, and I know that many other colleagues felt the same way too. But isn't that proof of an imagination placed in a straitjacket? Career pathways will do this to you. They harness your resources and channel them in one direction, just as canals are used to redirect the path of a river through a city. With locks and dams, we control the ebb and flow of the water to make it serve our purpose, but in so doing we temper its power. Remember when you go for a stroll by the canal how it was once a gushing river capable of flooding entire cities.

Likewise, career pathways temper our natural instincts and passions in order to shape us as professionals who fit neatly into an establishment. There are distinct advantages to this approach, but limitations too. Once the harness has been placed on you, you're no longer at liberty to skip about gleefully like the mustangs of the Wild West, but must channel your energies into serving the cause for which you've been commissioned. Also, your perspective may become so narrow that you won't know of any life other than that of the factory in which you were raised.

Managing your destiny

What then should be our response? We cannot leave our destiny to the education system, or else we'll find ourselves on a conveyor belt heading for a destination we don't want to go to. Getting off the belt may prove tricky, especially if it goes against expectations, and there's also the matter of recovering from any limitations the system might have placed on our thinking processes.

While you're still a child and under your parents' supervision, you might not be able to resist their attempts to steer you towards a career you don't want to pursue, but you don't have to abandon your dreams either. You can keep them alive by engaging in activities that fuel them. If the subject you're most interested in isn't in the school curriculum, then you ought to find ways to study it yourself. In the age of the internet, this couldn't be easier.

You can also ask your parents to provide you with opportunities for practical experience, and if they can't, start asking around. Conduct a Google search, speak to people who are already pursuing your interests, and ask them how you can do the same. For safety's sake, make sure your parents know what you're doing.

If you've left full-time education and are already working in a profession that is not aligned with your true destiny, then you should just hang in there for now and earn enough to pay your bills. At the same time, you should always keep your dream in view. Pursue it in your free time, not as a hobby but more intensively—as you would a second job.

If your job is so hectic as to afford you no time to pursue your dreams, then you ought to start thinking about a new job. Go for a position where you'll be able to learn and develop in the direction of your dreams. And if you can't find the right job, then go for one that's not too demanding. You want to be able to finish work and have enough time and energy to pursue your dreams.

Earning a high salary should not be your primary goal. Jobs with high pay are usually demanding, and the stress levels make it impossible to relax even when you're not at work. Some people worry about the next day's work while at home watching TV with their families. That's not a good job to have if you also want to follow your destiny. What you need is a job where you can walk away at the end of the day and have a free mind to think about the things that are important to you. That may mean a lower income, but you can supplement it with a passive income.

A passive income is the kind that doesn't require much effort to keep it coming in. It does require time and effort to set up, but after that, it doesn't take much to keep it going. Do an internet search on the topic, go on YouTube and you'll be amazed at the opportunities available. Read books on securing your financial future: here is one I can recommend: *The Richest Man in Babylon* by George S Clason.

The role of parents

Parents have a role in this too. As a parent, you cannot leave your child's future either to fate or to the education system. You must help them discover their purpose by encouraging them to pursue their interests and dreams. Every child has interests, passions and natural abilities. Together these things offer clues about a child's purpose. To ignore these clues is to ignore the child's destiny. As parents, our role is to guide and nurture our children as well as provide the conditions for them to flourish. This includes providing formal education, but the overarching goal must be to develop their potential.

To be useful guides to our children, we must know their interests and strengths and encourage them to develop in that direction. We mustn't merely slot them into a career pathway, as good as it may seem. We need to give consideration to the things that inspire them and provide them with opportunities to develop their talents and abilities. This will help them discover their purpose.

A child's interests may not be on the school curriculum, but that doesn't mean the child should give up on them. There are scholarships and sponsorship schemes both at the national and local council levels. There are also charities and NGOs that provide opportunities for children's development. The Prince's Trust in the UK is one such organisation, and there are many more, we just need to Google them, pick up the phone and speak to them. We need to be relentless in our desire to help our children develop.

We can only guide our children through the education system if we know how it works. Therefore, this is an area we need to take a keen interest in. We need to learn about the different career options and the opportunities and limitations that come with them. This way, we can become competent guides for our children.

Every now and again a young person with a dream will get restless and want to go off and pursue their dream. If their parents are unable to provide the right guidance, the child might feel the need to go and find someone who understands their aspirations. And the child will listen to them even if the person lacks the wisdom required to guide the child. We have a duty, therefore, to make sure our children get proper guidance. If we're unable to offer it ourselves, then we ought to find them a mentor. What we mustn't do is ignore the cries of their souls or worse still, shoot down their dreams. We must not, in an attempt to secure our children's financial future, shove them down a career pathway of our choice without due regard for their own dreams and aspirations.

Daddy, I quit

I once met a young man just as he was about to give up a career in dentistry. It wasn't that he hated being a dentist; he just couldn't identify with a profession that was entirely his parents' choice. He was fully aware of the financial rewards he was leaving behind, but that meant little in light of the feeling of dissatisfaction he felt each day. Everyone kept telling him what a bad idea it was to give up his career, and some wondered whether he was suffering from a nervous breakdown.

When he met me, he expected I'd echo those views, but instead, I told him how important it was to listen to the cries of his soul if he didn't want to have any regrets later. I then explained that when something is thrust on us, we end up developing an aversion to it. I encouraged him to set himself free from the obligation of pursuing a career in dentistry. This would liberate his mind and enable him to discover his true aspirations.

I also advised him not to burn all his bridges with the dental profession—then he could make a U-turn later if he did discover that dentistry really was for him after all. The look of relief on his face was unmistakable when he realised I wasn't going to condemn him as everyone else had.

This story shows just how crucial it is to avoid being driven merely by a desire to secure our children's future, as important as that is. The story also demonstrates the approach to take when children want to go off and do their own thing. Rather than stopping them, we ought to give them permission to do so and go alongside them in an advisory role. This way, they'll be more likely to listen to us.

Managing distractions

There comes a time when young people want to settle down and have a family. That's fine, but as we've explained already, it can kill your dreams. Marriage is a graveyard for dreams, though we may not want to believe it. Don't for a moment think you can just stroll in and still fulfil your dreams as planned. Ask people who are married to find out how many have managed to do so. The truth is that marriage places demands on you, including the need to please your spouse and provide for your family, and if you come from a culture with strong family traditions, then you also have to meet the expectations of your in-laws and the wider community.

It's hard to hold on to your dreams while surrounded by a sea of expectations and competing demands. And we make things harder for ourselves by starting badly. Many insist on an elaborate and costly wedding, forgetting that marriage is a marathon and that the wedding is merely the opening ceremony. The actual event begins after the honeymoon, but when the coffers have already been exhausted, the run will be harder to do.

Anyone who has run a marathon will tell you of the need to pace yourself and not expend all of your energies at the beginning, but that's what many people do in marriage. We pursue the initial stages so intensely that there's often little left to savour later. And it's in the early stages that dreams are lost—in the embrace of your loved one, nothing else seems to matter. But the day of reckoning soon arrives, forcing us to consider what we've done. This is why marriage ought to be planned. It doesn't sound romantic but then very little in life is.

Don't mortgage the rest of your life for a day's celebration. Don't pursue your relationships so vigorously that there's nothing to savour afterwards, and never lose sight of your dreams. You probably think this is only a man's perspective, but I know women who feel the same way too.

Plan your marriage, not just your wedding

Make sure that you're already on the path to fulfilling your dreams before you step into marriage. Find someone whose ambitions rhyme with yours; don't say "Yes" to the first good-looking person that comes along. Don't be smitten by someone's charm, flashy car, fat wallet or social standing. Don't merely focus on their "family man" or "wife material" appeal, as good as that may sound. Remember your dreams and don't allow yourself to be driven by your hormones. Look for someone who is purpose-driven and then ask: Am I comfortable with the direction that they're heading in? Is my vision compatible with theirs? Am I likely to fulfil my dreams if I join my life with theirs? Think about their destiny too and ask the same questions: How can I support my future spouse in accomplishing their purpose while fulfilling mine? Is this marriage going to end up derailing their goals and mine?

Discuss your vision

One of the easiest ways to know whether you've found the right person is to discuss your aspirations with them. If they look disinterested or seem as if they want to talk you out of pursuing your dreams, it's a sign that you haven't found the right person yet. Don't expect to be able to fulfil your ambitions while married to someone who isn't interested in them. Remember that your dreams are part of you. Even though the dreams may not be fully formed yet, they mustn't be ignored. So, talk about your vision and watch their reaction. They may not identify with it at first, which is ok, but you should keep mentioning the topic, and continue to observe their response. Make sure you keep this subject in the foreground throughout your courtship; otherwise it'll disappear in the multitude of problems that arise later.

Moreover, the only way for your future spouse to know that your dreams are important to you is for you to keep reminding them. Don't create the impression that you can do without them. If you do, then don't be surprised when your dreams disappear from the family agenda.

Key facts:

- Obstacles preventing us from pursuing our dreams exist in our immediate environment, in society at large, in the education system and in career pathways
- To realise your dreams, you must keep your sights set on them and remain focused
- It is your own responsibility, and not that of anyone else, for you to pursue your dreams
- Parents have a role in managing their children's dreams
- Parents can act as their children's career guides if they equip themselves with the right knowledge
- Take into consideration potential distractions when planning your life
- Plan your marriage not just your wedding

Some points to consider:

- What are your dreams?
- Where are you in the development of your dreams?
- Will your educational pursuits help to fulfil your purpose?
- How can you re-ignite your old dreams?
- How do you stay on track and avoid getting distracted?
- Do you know what your children's dreams are?
- Are you helping your children to develop and pursue their dreams?
- Are you equipped to act as your children's educational guide? If not, do you need to find them a mentor?

Chapter 7

Discover your assignment

When it comes to explaining our existence and purpose, the story of creation offers the clearest of accounts. In it, we're told how God created the heavens and earth. He also made the plants, the animals, and finally humans. The earth that God made was perfect, but it did not have everything. It had a garden, but it did not have gardening tools. It had trees but no houses, tables or chairs.

The first humans had able bodies and minds, but they didn't wear any clothes and didn't know an awful lot about their surroundings. In a nutshell, the earth had plenty of resources, but most of these were in a raw state, waiting to be tapped.

God charged the humans he'd created with the responsibility of managing the earth and its resources. His words were: "be fruitful and multiply, master (subdue) and replenish the earth." To master the earth, they'd need to first study it and develop the means to harness its resources. They'd also need to procreate, for only then could the whole earth be mastered.

As new generations appeared, they too would study a part of the earth that was of interest to them, and then work hard to harness and manage its resources. In other words, everyone would have a purpose; there would be a domain waiting to be mastered and taken care of, and it would be their job to find and fill that domain.

Everywhere you look today; you see this account of creation unfolding. Some people are interested in wildlife and study an aspect of zoology. Today, they're working as conservationists and university lecturers. Others have developed expertise in mining that they might tap the earth's mineral resources.

The first humans wouldn't have had many social problems to solve, but as the earth's population grew, such issues would have emerged and would have had to be addressed. Today there are such domains as healthcare, law and order, hospitality, entertainment and sanitation. All these have arisen in response to the earth's social and environmental problems. From the above, you can hopefully see that the story of creation offers a useful framework within which to evaluate the reason for our existence.

How to discover your domain

Nature doesn't make mistakes, so we have brains because we need to think, eyes because we need to see and talents to help us fulfil our assignment. Every natural endowment we possess serves a purpose, and our passions and interests are there for a reason too.

There's a reason for you getting upset about certain things when others can easily ignore the same problems. There's a reason for animal cruelty really bothering you, just as there is for lawlessness and lack of innovation, as well as for practically everything else. These are all domains to be mastered, and your concern is a clue that this may be your domain. You may not be a pioneer in it, but you can certainly bring about improvement.

Bill Gates created Windows, and that sparked a host of other inventions. Google probably wouldn't exist without it. Steve Jobs invented the iPhone, and that inspired others to develop incredible apps. There's always room for improvement, so if you're bothered by some technical problem and are technically gifted, you could start looking for a solution. Take time to study the issue. Study the solutions that are already there, and then see if you can create a better one or adapt what's already in existence.

Follow your passion

Are you passionate about animals? Do you get upset when you witness animal cruelty? I bet most of us do, but some people can't sleep for many days afterwards. Don't ignore the yearnings of your soul. There's a reason why merely sending money to an animal charity hasn't settled the concerns; your soul is trying to give you a clue about your assignment that you should act on. Don't just run in a marathon to raise money for an animal charity; go one step further: start studying the problem. Find out what drives cruelty to animals. Remember, only those who commit to studying a problem will find a solution.

Don't just discuss it with your friends, or go on protest marches. Look for books and other educational material on the topic. Join an online forum. Find out what others are already doing about it; meet with them, and learn from them. If you can't find anyone locally, consider travelling abroad. Meet with people from other countries, study their methods and if applicable, adopt them. Don't be passive—take an active stance!

The story of OXFAM

When a group of ordinary citizens gathered together in a church in the city of Oxford, little did they know that their actions would lead to so many changed lives. But 76 years later, this is what OXFAM has done. The acronym stands for Oxford Famine Relief Committee, which was set up in 1942 by a small group of locals. Their aim was to persuade the British government to allow food relief through the Allied blockade during the Greek Famine in 1942. Today OXFAM is the fourth largest charity in the UK with a budget of over £400 million; their interventions have eased suffering across the globe.

Obviously, OXFAM wouldn't be what it is today without the support of the general public, but it took the concerns of ordinary people to get the ball rolling. So, arise; you too can solve a problem.

Since writing this chapter, I see that OXFAM has been embroiled in a scandal about the behaviour of some of their workers. This is regrettable, but it doesn't take away from the noble aims of those who set up the organisation.

Be committed to solving a problem

Whatever your assignment is, it's going to involve some problem-solving. Every product or service solves a problem. Cars solve the problem of transportation, phones help with communication, and the postal service helps to deliver parcels. They each solve a problem. The company you work for solves a problem, and your job role is also about solving a problem. You may never be sure of your life's assignment, but if you commit to solving a problem, you won't be far off.

Case study: Thai cave rescue

In July 2018 the world watched as 12 boys and their football coach were rescued from the depths of a flooded cave in Thailand. It was a complex operation, deemed a miracle by some after it concluded successfully. But that miracle wouldn't have been possible without sacrifice, goodwill, cooperation and human ingenuity.

Outside the cave, parents waited anxiously for news about the stranded children. Inside, rescuers from different parts of the world worked tirelessly to locate the boys, Navy SEALs and civilian rescuers amongst them. The Thai government mobilised its resources and many other nations sent in help. Through their coordinated efforts, the boys and their coach were all rescued. There were no casualties except for one of the rescuers, a Thai Navy SEAL.

One of the foremost persons in the rescue operation was Dr Richard Harris, an Australian anaesthetist and a trained cave rescuer. He was on holiday when he heard about the boys' ordeal, and he left for Thailand without delay. He was one of the first to get to the boys, and he stayed with them treating their wounds and offering them reassurance. It was he who anesthetised them when the evacuation began.

Without his unique skill set (cave diving and specialist medical expertise) the rescue operation would not have been as successful as it was. As a matter of fact, when the British rescuers originally understood the task, they recommended Dr Harris knowing that his skills would come in handy.

Dr Harris is an example of someone who pursued his passion and put it to good use. A passion and a hobby for him, Dr Harris' cave diving proved lifesaving for others. This is why you mustn't neglect your true desires. Perhaps these desires will lead you to your true purpose on earth: to follow your passion and then be useful in helping others. Pursue it with intensity, but not selfishly, making your skills available for use when the need arises.

Don't live for yourself alone

There's a saying that goes like this: "if you're wrapped up in yourself, you make a small package." If your goal in life is to earn enough to pay your bills, you're limiting yourself. If you're living solely for you and your family's needs, then again, you're probably operating below your potential—animals do the same; indeed many do a better job than humans.

Birds, for instance, begin their day much earlier than us; they know that the early bird catches the worm. They also know that food won't come to them; they must go and find it.

Animals are often more committed to caring for their families than humans are. Emperor penguins, for instance, endure weeks of bitter cold on an empty stomach while they wait for their young ones to hatch. They know that the survival of the next generation depends on their efforts, and there are no orphanages or foster homes where they can dump their young ones and escape their responsibilities. Therefore, working hard to provide for your family, while important, is no big deal; it's your basic responsibility.

By the way, it's not absolutely necessary that you start a family; many people would be happier and live more meaningful lives if they remained single. However, if you do decide to raise a family, then it's worth making a good job of it. But this is no more than animals do; it doesn't make you special. You're human, you're superior to the animals, and you were created to pursue a much higher goal. Humans have been designed to do more than take care of their needs. We are the earth's managers and are here to bring solutions to the world's problems. So, start thinking big, and start thinking beyond your own daily existence.

Some of you may be thinking; "I'm so insignificant; how can I solve any of the world's problems." Others may be thinking that life is hard enough as it is. The last thing they want to do is add to their responsibilities. But such objections show you're missing the point: our assignments can sustain us, and also catapult us to greatness. To ignore them is to be short-sighted.

Everyone has an assignment, and that assignment is not about pleasing themselves. The ultimate goal in life is to find a solution to a problem; it's to put a smile on someone's face. Therefore, if you want to find your assignment, you must be committed to solving a problem and serving people.

If you live only to please yourself, you're wasting your life. If you're not living to solve a problem, then you haven't lived your life yet. When you're gone, no one will know that you were ever here. Commit yourself to solving a problem—that's the reason you were given thinking faculties. You were given this ability for more than just taking care of your own needs and those of your family.

The satisfaction you'll get from fulfilling your calling far exceeds that which comes from simply pleasing yourself. What joy, when you're able to look back and say, "I've done what I was sent here for, I've fought the good fight."

Live to solve a problem. Don't waste your life pleasing yourself.

Live for your assignment

When you're successful at a job interview, you develop hope, and when you land a new job, you get excited. But do you know what that hope is about? The chance comes to put your knowledge and expertise to good use by doing something you love. Money plays a role too, but if the job is related to your field of study or an area of interest, then the hope you feel is aspirational. It's linked to a cry from within your soul for self-expression.

But you start that job and soon realise that things aren't going to turn out as you'd imagined. Going to work becomes a drag, and the salary becomes the only thing to look forward to. But even that soon ceases to bring any excitement, because often, the money will have been earmarked for bills and other expenses even before it reaches your bank account. It doesn't take long before work begins to feel like a fraud, and you start to think you've been cheated. Many in this situation wake up each morning with a voice in their head screaming: No! No! No! But they don't have the guts to get off the hamster wheel.

Some in this situation look longingly to retirement for a much-needed respite and a chance to do the things they really love —but why would you sign off the most productive years of your life to your employer while you pick up the scraps? Don't get me wrong, you can still be productive after retirement as many are; but the point is; why would you devote the prime of your life to something you can barely tolerate in the hope that you can go on and do the things you enjoy doing after you're finally set free? Why not buck that trend, get in touch with your dreams and live as you've always wanted to? If your heart yearns for self-expression, why not make that a reality? Don't continue in a job you hate, and where opportunities for development are non-existent. One day you'll look back and regret it. Start the process of change now! Start living for your assignment; start answering the calls of your soul! Break the cycle of monotony!

If you hate your job despite being paid a handsome salary, then you're probably not on the path to your destiny. If your work fails to inspire you, and you're merely working to pay your bills, again, you've probably strayed from your assignment. But if you commit the rest of your life to discovering and fulfiling your calling, you'll find the satisfaction you crave.

This kind of satisfaction is what Henry Ford, Thomas Edison, Mother Theresa, Cecil Jackson-Cole (co-founder of OXFAM), Henry Dunant and Gustave Moynier (founders of the Red Cross), George Washington Carver, Nelson Mandela and many others would have known. Not many other people have ever enjoyed that feeling. There's also a sense of fulfilment that Bill Gates, Bono, Sir Bob Geldof, Mark Zuckerberg, and other less well-known people must feel but that most have yet to experience. But you don't have to remain among the majority;

you can take a decision today to be different, to discover your purpose and live for your destiny.

You've been wired for your assignment

When you discover your purpose, you'll also realise that you've been wired for that very thing. Your body, intellect, temperament, talents and interests are all there to help you fulfil your task. Your assignment will maximise your potential and stretch your imagination. If you feel underused, it's a sign that you haven't yet found the thing you were sent here for. Get in touch with your assignment and watch things change.

Many of us apply for jobs hoping they'll bring fulfilment when what we need to do is discover our assignment and then find a position to help us fulfil it. And if finding your calling proves a challenge, then just follow your passion. Find a job that is related to your interests and taps into your natural abilities. This will afford you the opportunity for self-expression and help develop your potential. If you're in a job that isn't related to your assignment and offers few opportunities for professional development, then do what you have to do; stay there and earn a salary. Learn what you can while you're there, but keep thinking about what you want to do with your life. Think of a problem to solve, a domain you could master, and then develop a strategy to move onto the path of destiny.

Key facts:

- Everyone has an assignment or calling
- Your assignment is to solve a problem
- The clues to your calling are the things that upset you, the things you're passionate about and the things that stir your imagination.
- Your assignment is not to please yourself or even look after your family
- Catering for your family's needs is your basic responsibility
- Live for something bigger than yourself
- You'll not find greater happiness than in fulfilling your purpose

Some points to consider:

- Why are you on earth? What is your assignment?
- What are you passionate about?
- What problem often upsets me?
- Are you satisfied with where your life is heading?
- Are you fulfilling your potential?

Chapter 8

Unleashing your potential

Sarah and Andy, the characters we introduced at the beginning, are different in many ways, especially in the degree to which they have developed themselves. Andy is fortunate to have had parents who cared about his personal development and who also had the means to make it happen. They may not have understood the importance of letting him pursue his passion, but they did an excellent job of helping him develop as a human being. They taught him such virtues as diligence, perseverance, and self-control, which have made him into the conscientious father, husband and employee that he is.

Andy's first-class education has contributed further to his personal growth and has harnessed his potential; although it must be said, only to a limited degree. We can only maximise our potential when we discover our true assignment and start pursuing our dreams.

Sarah, on the other hand, is like a rough diamond buried deep beneath the earth's surface. She has lots of potential, but no one knows about it. The gem must be dug out, cleaned and polished that its beauty may be manifest to all. Sarah needs to discover what resources nature has given her, and develop them. This is going to be crucial to her fulfilling her dreams.

Discover the tools for your assignment

When people hear the word *resource*, they often think of money or material possessions. Perhaps, this is why many consider themselves to be unfortunate. But if we are to fulfil our potential, we must see beyond the limitations that a lack of money brings. We may not have much money, but nature has given us other resources to help us fulfil our calling, and it's up to us to find and develop them.

Where are my resources?

We have two kinds of resources: our primary resources are our body, brain, personality, talent, time and the ability to work. We can also acquire secondary resources in the form of knowledge, skills, money and assets.

We're born with our primary resources, but the secondary resources, which lie within the environment, must be acquired. You may deem yourself less privileged in life, but unless you suffer from an illness and are severely incapacitated, you're probably rating yourself on secondary rather than primary resources.

Anything that doesn't grow dies

The second truth we need to know about resources is that they need nurturing. In life, anything that doesn't grow dies, and things decrease in value over time unless they're maintained and updated. A car bought today will not be worth the same amount in 5 years. Unless it's a vintage classic, a collector's item, its value will depreciate over time, and it will eventually need to be scrapped. Money that isn't invested soon decreases in value; inflation eats into its value. And a business that stops growing will eventually collapse.

This principle applies to nature as well. Every human begins life as a single cell, a product of fusion between a sperm cell and an egg cell. That cell grows and multiplies, producing other cells which also give rise to new cells. The process of growth and multiplication continues until there is a tissue mass. The different cells in this tissue mass differentiate or specialise into organs, organ systems and then a body. We each come into the world as babies but do not stay that way. We grow physically and mentally to become adults, and when we stop growing, we start dying slowly.

It's the same with plants. Plants grow daily, and when they stop growing, they begin their slow march towards death. What's the message here? Growing is how we stay alive, and to remain where we are in life, we must keep improving ourselves. If we don't, then the law of depreciation will catch up with us.

Progress isn't optional; it's essential. Seeking to be better isn't reserved for the ambitious, it's what nature does all the time and what we must do too. We need to be on our toes, growing what we have, investing our money, keeping our bodies in shape, learning new things, and keeping the knowledge we already have fresh in our minds. Only then will we make the most of our lives.

We're all capable of achieving success, but we need to keep improving ourselves and multiplying what we have. If a farmer stops complaining about his lack of means and plants the few seeds he has, he'll have a harvest. If he keeps back some of the crop for planting in the next season, he'll have another harvest. If he keeps increasing the quantity of seed sown, he'll gradually increase his wealth.

Don't underestimate your resources

You can become great and have plenty, by growing the seeds you have. And you always have resources that you can multiply even if you're broke and live in a developing country. You can grow your net worth even if you're in prison.

Prisons are some of the best places on earth for personal development. There, you have two of the essential ingredients in abundance; time and solitude. People on the outside have to factor other people into their time. If they're married, they must devote some of their time to their families. Their friends will also take out a slice, as will churches or other religious organisations. Some of the time will be spent on recreation, and if they have a job, then their employers will also take out massive chunks, leaving very little time for personal development. In fact, any free time may well be spent worrying about how they're going to make it to the end of the month.

But if you're in prison, you're away from all that. There's a routine, but it takes up very little time, so the rest of the time is for you to use as you please, and you can choose to spend it developing yourself into the person you want to be. Rather than sitting in your cell all day ruing past mistakes and wishing you had acted more wisely, why not use the time to develop yourself? Consider your prison sentence a chance to redeem yourself. Make it your goal to come out of jail a different person.

This is what Nelson Mandela did. Being in prison gave him an opportunity to reflect, and he concluded that he wanted to live a very different life if he was ever released. He'd been locked up with no hope of ever getting out, and there were limits to the amount of mail he could receive, so he didn't know that momentum was building up outside for his release.

Mandela chose to develop himself purely on the basis that it was the right thing to do, and prison gave him plenty of opportunity to do so. There was ample time to ponder his life in solitude, and among some notorious prison wardens. Their attitudes could easily have been a source of discouragement, but Mandela saw this as an opportunity to develop his character.

The people who oppose us can actually be the best resources we have, although we often don't see it that way. By their antagonism, they help us to develop temperance, which is an essential trait to have if you want to be a leader. In Mandela's case, his temperance would mark him out as an outstanding leader. He left prison as the most qualified person to liberate South Africa from apartheid. Many opposed his efforts, and if he hadn't learnt temperance in jail, he might have resorted to something other than the peaceful means he deployed.

Sarah can begin her personal development in prison. She needn't wait till her release. She can take advantage of the educational courses and job opportunities that many prisons offer. She should also become a more prolific reader, and frequent the prison library because personal growth is virtually impossible without knowledge.

Development starts wherever you are and with what you have

Prisons can help you develop your character, but you don't have to go to jail to succeed—you can achieve success wherever you are if you embrace the same principles. So, don't just sit there wishing for better conditions; do something with what you have! Don't let your limitations hold you back, Remember that there are always resources that can help you develop. You have a body, a personality, intellect and talent.

Arnold Schwarzenegger would not be where he is today if he hadn't developed his body. He started out with bodybuilding. This then got him a role in a film, and his fame as an actor got him elected as governor of California. If you study his career carefully, you'll see that none of this could have happened if he hadn't taken up bodybuilding. He started with what he had, and you can see where it got him. Likewise, *you* have to begin with what you have.

You may not have abundant resources, but you have yourself, and often, that's enough. You may be feeling hamstrung by your lack of means, but look again, and you'll discover plenty of opportunities. Determine your goals and then decide on the best way to achieve them.

Do you want to be a bodybuilder? Don't be deterred by the lack of gyms in your area, and the same applies if you want to be an athlete. Julius Yego is probably a household name for athletics fans, although you probably won't have heard of him if athletics is not your thing. Coming from Kenya, it is perhaps unsurprising that he should be an Olympic medallist. After all, Kenyans are good at athletics, aren't they? **Newsflash**—no Kenyan had ever won a medal in any international competition in javelin before Yego. The might of that African athletic powerhouse is in long-distance running rather than in field events. Julius Yego was the first to win a field event, and the remarkable thing is that he did it without a coach. He perfected his technique while watching YouTube videos. He started with what he had.

After coming first in the Kenyan national championship, he went on to win the javelin throw in the All-Africa Games in 2011 and came fourth in the World Championships two years later. The following year, Yego became the first Kenyan to win a Commonwealth Games gold medal in a field event. A year later he was the world champion.

When I was a child, my parents couldn't afford to buy me many of the toys and gadgets I wanted, and I may have considered myself less privileged than some of my peers. But all that would change after I made a new friend. He and his brother didn't have any toys either, but unlike me, they didn't see it as a problem. Using easily accessible materials, they made any toy or gadget they wanted; so off I went with them on an adventure. Together, we made toy cars from flattened milk tins and cut the wheels out of old flip-flops. We made makeshift skating boards from wood and any other materials we could lay our hands on. We rolled old car tyres around and gleefully chased after them. A lack of the usual resources didn't hold us back, and neither must you let your limitations stop you. Get thinking and construct a gym from local materials if you want to be a bodybuilder. Use the internet to research bodybuilding. Find out what types of weights you need and make them from the materials around you. Be innovative, and don't let your circumstances hold you back!

Do you wish to return to full-time education? Do you feel hindered by the lack of educational opportunities where you live? If so, cheer up; learning isn't what it used to be. You don't have to step into a classroom to be educated. As a matter of fact, you may find the classroom experience somewhat frustrating if you have a voracious appetite for knowledge. In school, you'd have to adhere to a curriculum designed with little consideration for your individual curiosities and unique abilities.

But outside the education system, you can be master of your own destiny. You can choose any subject you want, and prioritise the topics that will help you fulfil your purpose. You can also allow your appetite for knowledge to lead you, and proceed at your own pace. This is how many successful people live—they take charge of their education. There aren't many university graduates with first-class degrees among millionaires, you know. Many dropped out of the education system, but then took charge of their learning, and have since become very successful.

You too can be successful in your life, but you must take charge of your destiny first. Start today by getting access to the internet. If you live in the developed world, this shouldn't be a problem—there's free internet everywhere: in libraries, restaurants and hotel lobbies, for example. There are also websites offering free books including https://www.pdfdrive.net. Visit these websites and start learning. Determine what you need to know and then begin the process.

Access to libraries may be limited in developing countries, but there are British Council libraries dotted around the world, and these are a good source of free educational material. They also offer free internet access and newspapers to keep you up-to-date with world events. Additionally, you can find American centres, as well as Alliance Francaise if you prefer to read in French. These centres tend to be located in the capital or other major cities, so if you live in a remote area, you'll need to make your way to a city to access knowledge—but don't let this become a stumbling block. Where there's a will, there's a way. Focus your mind, be determined and you'll find the resources you need to improve yourself.

Catch a vision of your future self

Imagine being a member of the royal family of your country and the next in line to the throne. Your father, the present monarch is ill and isn't expected to live for very long. Therefore, those in charge of your father's household are frantically getting you prepared to succeed him. The future looks certain; you'll be king unless something unexpected happens, but the kind of ruler you'll be is far from settled. A lot depends on what you do with your life between now and the time of your accession to the throne.

You need to work hard to make yourself into the king the nation expects to have. This will involve developing character traits such as temperance, resilience, steadfastness, honesty and humility, to mention but a few. All these qualities are going to be needed in the future, and you must start acquiring them now so that you'll be ready when duty calls. Otherwise, you'll be a disappointment—you'll step into your father's shoes, but you won't be the king that everyone, including yourself, will have been hoping for. This, in essence, is what personal development is all about. It's about catching a vision of your future self and then working your way towards it. As in the above example, you need to work hard to develop traits that your future self will need to exhibit. If you fail to act, a different future will await.

Most people understand the role of education in personal development, but they fail to see the importance of having the right character traits. And yet without these, success can be elusive. Personal development therefore not only involves the acquisition of knowledge and expertise, but also the shaping of your character traits. Only then will you be guaranteed to make a success of the opportunities that will come your way.

Each one of us can live a fulfilled life, but the path to this life lies through personal growth. A bright future awaits, but you won't find it unless you develop yourself. If you sit there waiting for success to happen, you'll be disappointed. Arise now and create the future you desire!

> *"Man's main task is to give birth to himself, to become what he potentially is. This most important product of his effort is his own personality."*

> Erich Fromm

You need good examples

To achieve your aim, you sometimes need a guide, and the best person to guide you is someone who's been there and done it already; someone who has accomplished what you want to achieve. Study their lives, find out what makes them tick and how they got to where they are. Discover the principles they found to be most helpful and consider incorporating some of them into your own life.

If you aspire to be a leader, then start learning from great leaders. Read the biographies of Nelson Mandela, Margaret Thatcher, Winston Churchill, Martin Luther King and Benjamin Franklin. Lay aside your reservations for a moment and find out what made these leaders great. Not everything about their lives will be worth imitating, but effective people often have habits that are worth emulating.

Benjamin Franklin's biography is particularly noteworthy. From an early age, he had a great sense of his own somebodiness, but he also understood that he would not attain the heights he craved without developing himself. He opted to become a vegetarian in his teens so he could purchase books with the money he saved from not buying meat. He was a prolific reader. He also undertook to develop a set of character traits that he thought would help him in the future. He's one of the pioneers of personal development as we now know it.

Don't give up hope

Harnessing your potential is only possible if you believe that something positive will come of your life. This is why you must eliminate the word *hopeless* from your vocabulary. If there's no hope, then find it. Look for the silver lining—there's bound to be one.

Conventional wisdom says it's best not to set your hopes too high in case they get dashed. But hope only fails if we fail to act. There are two ways to approach hope: we can choose to be passive and wait for our wishes to be fulfilled, or we can work hard to achieve the things we hope for. The latter is never a bad idea.

Hope keeps us going. When we have it, we have a reason to live, to work hard, and to be successful. When we lose hope, we lose the motivation to keep pushing forward, and we eventually give up; even though our redemption might be just around the corner. This reminds me of the story of the Chilean miners who got stuck 700 metres below ground after the walls of the mines collapsed. Rescuers set to work immediately, but they hit an obstacle when another cave-in blocked access to the place the miners were in. Drilling equipment was sent in from around the world, but the first couple of attempts yielded no results. And as time went by, the hope of finding the miners alive began to slip away. The families of the trapped miners were unyielding though and kept up pressure for rescue efforts to continue.

As for the miners, they'd survived the collapse and were doing their best to stay alive eating tiny portions of food each day, drinking dirty water and propping each other up emotionally in the hope that something would happen. They had every reason to give up hope but chose not to. Help did come eventually: the rescuers managed to drill down to where the miners were, and after so many days found them all alive and well. How did that happen? Hope!

If the families had given up hope, rescue efforts might have ended sooner, and the miners might not have survived. Likewise, if the miners had given up hope they might have finished their food supplies and died of starvation before the rescuers got to them. Their belief that they'd come out alive led to action that was eventually rewarded. So hope can be something very positive, especially when you're prepared to do what it takes to make your hopes materialise. You may not see any results for a while, but if you persevere, your efforts might just be rewarded. You need hope and plenty of it, and don't be passive; let your hope drive you towards action.

Hope fails only if we remain passive.

Tribute to a fighter

I'm reminded of my good friend, Dr Solomon Adinortey Dogbe. He is now no longer with us, but his life was an embodiment of the principle of never giving up. Growing up in his native Ghana, there was an awful lot that he couldn't take for granted, not even primary education. Yet he managed to complete secondary school and gain entry into a sixth-form college.

Solomon's dream was to study medicine, but with the competition for places in the state medical schools being so fierce he knew he had to look elsewhere. But where? He couldn't travel abroad to study as the cost was beyond his means.

Solomon needed to know if there were scholarships available, but even this information was difficult to find. There was no internet then, so he couldn't just Google it. As luck would have it, he bumped into a friend who had the answers he was after. There were indeed scholarships on offer that could enable him to study medicine in Eastern Europe.

Only a small number of scholarships were available though, and hundreds of applicants were competing for only a few places. Besides, the selection process was well underway, so it was too late to apply.

Never one to be fazed by setbacks, Solomon determined that there must be another way to achieve his dream. And as they say, fortune favours the brave. One day he bumped into an attaché at the Polish Embassy and explained his situation. To cut a long story short, he learned that it was possible to gain admission to a university in Eastern Europe without going through the selection process in Ghana. This, however, meant paying for his education. Solomon decided to apply. Accepted by a medical school in Poland, he then had some "luck" with his airfare and made his way there.

When I first met Solomon, he'd just arrived in Lodz. He didn't know how he was going to get through the first year, having arrived without money for his tuition fees, but he seemed totally unperturbed, which is probably the thing I found most endearing about him. Instead, he told me about the obstacles he'd overcome to get to where he was. He was sure there'd be a way to fund his education.

Solomon had arrived in Poland without his luggage, which at first seemed like a significant setback, but the airline was going to deliver it several days later and pay him compensation. That money would come in handy as he'd arrived in Poland with hardly a penny in his pocket.

He'd found a way to pay for his first year's tuition when an old acquaintance who happened to be in Lodz at the same time stepped in to help. But the second year fee was a much larger sum, and it seemed that this time his game was up.

He was threatened with expulsion from the university, but then fate came to his rescue once again. He bumped into a professor who happened to know the Dean of the faculty of medicine. When the professor heard Solomon's story, he was moved with compassion and told the dean about it. The Dean presented Solomon's case to the university board, which granted him a discretionary waiver.

Solomon's life was full of good fortune, and yet nothing rolled into his lap. He had to work hard and take his chances. He was always out there, looking for opportunities to develop himself. Sometimes, it seemed that his game was up, and many, in his shoes, would have thrown in the towel. But quitting, for him, wasn't an option.

Not only did he complete his medical degree, but Dr Dogbe, as Solomon became known, also went on to set up a business before his life came to an abrupt end in 2016. He didn't stick around to reap the rewards of all his efforts, unfortunately, but he left behind a legacy that will be remembered for years to come. His story is proof that if you persevere, you might just get what you want.

Ralph Waldo Emerson is credited with the following truism:
When you take a decision, the universe conspires to make it happen.
How true!

You too can make it if you take that crucial decision not to give up on your dreams. So strengthen those feeble hands and the knees that give way easily. Lift up your head and begin looking for opportunities for personal development. The universe will conspire to reward your efforts.

Key facts:

- Everyone has potential
- To harness your potential, you must discover your resources and catch a vision of your future self
- A resource is anything that can be used to achieve your goals
- Resources must be developed and multiplied
- Personal development involves education
- You need hope to harness your potential
- Development starts at the place you're in, and with what you have
- Prison can be the perfect place for personal development

Some points to consider:

- What resources do you have for your assignment?
- Have you been developing your resources or neglecting them?
- How can you develop your resources further?
- What are you capable of becoming if you apply yourself?
- Ask yourself what's stopping you from realising your potential— think about fear, other people's opinions, and having no vision of your future self.
- How do you harness your potential?

Chapter 9

The body as a resource

Before I started writing this book, I'd never thought of my body as anything other than an earth suit; something meant to support my life. And I'm pretty sure I wasn't alone in my thinking. We all take our bodies for granted, and although it isn't good to focus too much on yourself, you cannot neglect your body either. We all need to take care of our body, and the day it stops functioning, we'll lose the right to be counted among the living.

Without your body, you wouldn't be here. No one would give you a job, conduct business with you or make friends with you. Having a body makes all that possible. You may not like yours much, or you may even detest some parts of it. You may have looked in the mirror and said: "yuck!" But that body you despise guarantees you many of the rights and privileges that you enjoy on earth, and the day you lose it, you'll also lose those privileges. Now, let's take a look at some of them.

Legitimacy

Having a body gives you the right to be here. The last time I checked, ghosts didn't have this right. It also gives you visibility and being visible means you can't be ignored. Now, some of you are probably thinking: "Wait a minute, I've been ignored many times." And you may be right, you may have endured the painful experience of being overlooked, but you can't be ignored; at least not indefinitely. If you were sitting in a café hours after finishing your drink, the staff would act as if you weren't there, but one of them would come to inform you if they were about to close the shop. They knew you were there all the time, but just didn't pay you any attention, and there's a difference. If there was a fire, everybody would have to be accounted for, including you. And that's because your body gives you legitimacy.

A right to privacy

Having a body gives you something called personal space. Though not clearly defined in law, this space entitles you to some privacy, and if someone encroached it without your permission, express or implied, they'd be breaching your privacy. If they acted in an intimidating manner, they could be liable to prosecution even though they hadn't touched you. But you wouldn't be entitled to this space if you didn't have a body. Your body defines where that space is, wherever you are.

Physical abilities

Your body enables you to perform physical tasks. You have this wonderful resource if you're able-bodied, and you probably have it too if you are disabled. Disabled people can often do things that able-bodied people can't do because physical disability often leads to compensation. People who suffer from visual impairment develop a keen sense of hearing, for example, and those without hands can do incredible things with their feet. Sometimes, they end up having the edge over able-bodied people in some areas of life. If you don't believe it, watch the Paralympics.

We all have this incredible resource called a body, the capabilities of which we have yet to fully discover. It doesn't matter if some parts are missing. There's a lot of reserve built into the body, and if we focus on developing what's left even after a life-changing accident, we'll be amazed at what we can achieve.

I've seen several documentary films about people who only took up sport after an accident that left them disabled. Before the accident, they took their bodies for granted, but after losing a limb, in some cases both, they began to discover the body's capabilities. And by developing those capabilities, some have become celebrities. No one knew who they were when their bodies were intact. This is why we needn't despair over our imperfect bodies.

Living in a material world

Your body allows you to operate in the physical world. Without it, you couldn't touch or be touched, and you couldn't eat or drink. You couldn't work, marry or have children. Life on earth would be impossible without a body, so you should recognise your body as a resource, and treat it as such. Let this truth sink in, and you'll want to start taking good care of your body.

The appendix has a purpose

The appendix is a small appendage at the end of the colon. Until recently doctors couldn't identify its purpose, and thought of it merely as a vestigial organ; meaning that its purpose had been rendered redundant through evolution. This seemed to make sense, as people whose appendices had been removed appeared not to suffer any consequences. But now doctors have discovered that the appendix does indeed play a vital role in the immune system.

The truth is that every part of the body serves a purpose, and the various attributes such as height, size, hair-length and eye colour all afford certain advantages. Being tall gives you the edge in basketball but so does being short. Tall players can make shots and blocks more easily, but their shorter teammates can often manoeuvre the ball better because of their lower centre of gravity.

With a height of 1.6 metres, Tyrone 'Muggsy' Bogues shouldn't have stood a chance in a sport where the average player is over 2 metres tall, and yet he was one of the most celebrated NBA players of his time. His short stature should have been a handicap, but it turns out that if we work with whatever nature has given us, we can succeed where no one expects us to. And if we work even harder, we may achieve "the impossible". With a vertical leap of 110 metres, Mugsy Bogues even managed to block the 2.13 metre Patrick Ewing from making a basket. This happened on 14 April 1993.

Mugsy didn't despise what nature gave him and neither must you. Work hard, and you'll be amazed at what you can achieve.

What's true of height is true of every attribute of the body. Your body is a resource, and you have to find the best way of putting it to use. Everything in your body is an asset, so you should stop seeing it merely as your earth suit. All the different intricacies and quirks in your body are there for a reason. There's a reason why your legs are shaped the way they are; it's not just a freak of nature. Start thinking differently about your body, and you'll begin to unlock its potential.

Take an inventory

Now you know that your body is an asset, start noting down its features. Note down your height, your size, the length of your hair and the colour of your eyes, etc. Record this information but don't evaluate it. Don't think of any feature as being good or bad, just record it. Next, ask yourself whether you look like someone famous.

When Minyong's colleagues started poking fun at him for looking like Kim Jong-Un, Minyong didn't find it funny. But after leaving military school, he decided to exploit his natural resemblance to the Supreme Leader of North Korea. He had a haircut, bought himself a cheap black suit, and set off for Seoul's trendy Hongdae district, and the rest, as they say, is history. "When I go downtown, I usually dress up as Kim Jong-Un because I'll be so popular that I won't need to take my wallet. Bar owners always give me free food and drinks," he says.

And Minyong's story doesn't end there—he went on to negotiate a contract with KFC to shoot a commercial. He could have been really bombed out by being compared with the North Korean dictator, but instead, saw an opportunity.

For a Vladimir Lenin lookalike, on the other hand, it all started when a group of tourists asked for a photo with him. They thought he looked like Lenin, the Russian revolutionary. That idea of a resemblance had crossed his mind before, but he hadn't made much of it. Hearing it from the mouth of complete strangers though, he decided to act. The lookalike started dressing up as Lenin and learnt a few of the politician's speeches and mannerisms. When I saw him, he was making a good living by frequenting tourist attractions in Moscow and having photoshoots with tourists. Here's someone who can think on his feet. And if he continues like this and takes some acting classes, he could land a role in a movie.

What you do with the assets nature has given you is entirely up to you. You can get upset about your body features or agonise about the talents you don't have, or you can think of ways to make the most of what you do have. So, take a good look at yourself; check out your head, neck, chest, waist and legs. Ask yourself whether you've got any stand-out features. Has anyone ever commented on any parts of your body?

Then move on to your personality traits. Ask yourself how other people describe you. If you're not sure how to answer that question, ask people who know you. Once you've completed your inventory, start thinking of how to make the most of your unique features.

Get rid of your complexes

The body is a marvel. The bones in your arms have ball-like ends that fit perfectly into sockets on adjacent bones to form joints. The two ends of the bones forming a joint are connected by ligaments that hold them in place, and they're surrounded by a sac of fluid for protection. This sac serves as a lubricant and shock absorber, thereby reducing the likelihood of injuries. Each joint is operated by muscles, and there are different types of joints with varying ranges of motion.

This perfection does not exist in the musculoskeletal system alone; it is found throughout the body. The whole body is fitted very neatly together in a perfect work of art and engineering. Some people suffer from illnesses that mar the expression of the original design, but we're all partakers of this perfection to some degree, and it enables us to do what we've been sent here to do. Therefore don't worry about the imperfections in your body. You do have something going for you. We have all been packaged and sent to earth on an assignment, so you have your own resources, and they're fit for your purpose. Value what you have, and stop seeing yourself as being disadvantaged. Start treating your standout features as a resource.

Do you have dwarfism? Don't worry about it—treat it as an asset.

There are disadvantages to being short, but there are advantages too. Learn to dwell on the latter. Focus your mind on the positives, and you'll end up projecting a positive image of yourself that will affect other people's attitudes towards you. Generally, people treat you according to how you come across and handle yourself. If you accept yourself and hold your head up high, they'll treat you as they do everyone else.

On the other hand, if you're very self-conscious, always trying to hide away your disability, you'll end up drawing attention to it. So, stop hiding, turn on the swagger, and don't wait for others to accept you. Lead the way, and they'll follow.

Do you have an illness? Don't pay too much attention to it. Get all the treatment you can and maximise your pain-free days by doing something productive and something you love. Switch on positivity! Don't let a victim mentality kick in. If you do, you'll end up neglecting your personal development.

Take good care of your body

To make the most of your life, you need a healthy body, so take good care of yours. Eat healthily and don't over-indulge. Avoid excesses. Such behaviour puts a strain on the body. Learn time management—it will take the stress out of your life. Learn to prioritise and set yourself free from others' opinions. Live happily—the happier you are, the healthier you'll be. Treat your body well, and it will last you longer.

Dr Phil Hammond, doctor and comedian recommends doing 9 things if you want to stay healthy and happy, he calls them CLANGERS:

Connect (with people)

Learn new things and continually challenge yourself

(Be) Active—engage in regular exercise

Notice the world around you and savour its riches

Give back to your community (and to the world at large [my addition])

Eat well

Relax

Sleep

I agree with him, these practices in the right proportions will help you maintain good health. Think of how you can incorporate CLANGERS into your life!

Don't abuse your body

When you don't know the purpose of a thing, abuse is inevitable. These are the words of the late Dr Myles Munroe. I travelled abroad recently and was shocked to see what little regard people have for their bodies. I heard story after story about people chasing a certain look and putting their bodies through extremes to achieve it. Let me clarify that these individuals weren't suffering from body dysmorphic disorder. There was no medical justification for their behaviour. Some were taking prescription drugs; others had undergone surgical procedures by unqualified practitioners. "Why would anyone want to do that?" I wondered. But then I remembered that this problem is not limited to certain parts of the world; it's also right here on our own doorstep.

We're all either trying to lose weight ourselves, or we know someone who is—maintaining a healthy weight has become one of the big preoccupations of our generation. But many approach it from the wrong angle. Weight gain comes from frequent overeating and too little physical activity. Reverse that pattern, and you'll lose weight. Sustainable weight loss comes through gradual lifestyle modifications, and a change in lifestyle means a shift in mindset; it means that your attitude towards food and exercise needs to change.

Many people approach eating like it's a major event; they go for it, and if there's plenty to eat, they gorge themselves. But the real purpose of food is to maintain a healthy body. It's ok to enjoy a treat from time to time, but we cannot overindulge and still expect to have healthy bodies. And some of us think we can cheat the system by going on a diet afterwards, but without a change in mindset, we're bound to put the weight back on.

Besides, to attempt losing weight through dieting alone is tackling the problem from only one angle. This usually leads to extreme dieting because of the need to compensate for the lack of exercise. But isn't this a form of self-inflicted torture?

Cherish what you have

Being alive and healthy are two of our bottom-line resources. While we're alive, we can dream and work hard to fulfil our dreams. We can attain great heights and contribute our share to making the world a better place. Being alive means, we can improve our situation. Death will close off that opportunity one day, but as long as we're here, we can make things better.

You may be overweight, have a pot belly, a bald head, and bags under your eyes. You may lack many of the qualities that society tells us are desirable, or you may even possess some of the traits that it frowns upon, but if you're alive and kicking, you're good to go. Don't let someone else's opinions drive you towards extreme behaviour. Delight in what you have! If you're lucky enough to have perfect health, then rejoice; but you don't need that to be a success. If your body still works, then you've got something going for you—your illness hasn't taken away everything. Start rejoicing now and don't wait for perfection—you already have two of life's bottom-line resources.

Key facts:

- Everyone has potential; no one came to this earth empty-handed
- Being alive and healthy are two of our most important resources
- Your physical attributes are also a resource
- Even if your body is imperfect, you still have a resource
- The poor and the rich both have the resource of a body
- Your body needs taking care of
- Don't abuse your body
- Start appreciating what you have; your body is a resource
- You don't need a perfect body to be a success

Some points to consider:

- Do you treat your body with respect?
- Do you look after your body?
- Have you been abusing your body?

Are you on a diet? If so, why? Are you doing it to please someone else?

Chapter 10

Press that button, turn on the magic

The brain is probably the most potent of all nature's endowments. Its capabilities are unmatched, and our other resources pale in comparison. Through the power of the mind, we can *see* that which cannot be seen, *hear* what cannot be heard, and travel to places beyond the reach of the body to create a new future for ourselves.

With the intellect, we can work out solutions to problems, including those we've never come across before. Our capacity for analytical thinking enables us to break down problems into smaller parts and look for patterns. We are also able to synthesise different pieces of information, some from distant memory, and create scenarios. We have this incredible resource at our disposal, and yet so many of us run off to other people for help when we encounter a problem. We forget that we too have a powerhouse within us and that all we need to do is switch it on.

Thinking is your number one resource

The earth, when it was formed, was not without problems. It was perfect but in a raw state. The diamonds were unpolished, and the iron was buried in ore, deep in the earth. The tables were hidden in the trees and the houses in the raw materials. Everywhere you looked, there were problems to solve, but He who created the universe was not bothered by this, knowing that he'd also given mankind the key to solving every single problem.

The ability to think critically isn't reserved for a privileged few—we all have it. Having that ability allows us to wriggle out of every problem we find ourselves in. It's through the power of thought that great inventions and discoveries are made. Discovering the laws of motion and gravity were both the result of thought. Knowledge of these laws has transformed our understanding of the world around us and has enabled people to make inventions and prevent accidents.

When asked how he arrived at the theory of gravity, Sir Isaac Newton replied: "by thinking about it continuously". He also said this about himself: "If I have done the public any service, it is due to my patient thought." Newton saw the ability to think as his number-one resource, and thinking his number-one activity.

Thinking is work

Thinking is the hardest work there is; which is probably the reason why so few engage in it.

This statement, often attributed to Henry Ford contains undeniable truth. Thinking, especially goal-directed thinking is hard work. It involves going down many alleys, and not knowing where they lead. Sometimes you have to discover the dead ends before finding what you're looking for. This is the hard part, and many of us give up after a few tries. But if we want to make the most of this marvellous resource that nature has given us, we mustn't ever give up. Each time we come to a dead end, we have to turn round, retrace our steps and start again. We must keep our eyes on the rewards, and those are plentiful. We should also enjoy the process as much as we desire the outcome. It's good to be curious and meticulous, covering all the bases. If you follow these steps, you'll soon be thinking like a genius. The difference between most of us and the genius is that we give up too soon.

Productive thinking doesn't come easily

We all do a lot of thinking every day, but most of it is circular and unproductive. We ruminate about our mistakes and mishaps and worry all day about things we have little control over. These negative thought patterns seem entrenched and are often our default mode. As a consequence, the powerhouse of the mind is rarely put to good use.

There's a way to think if we want to get results. Firstly, productive thinking doesn't come alone, we need to be *intentional* about it. Secondly, we need to tune out of every other thing as we focus our minds on the issue of interest to us. This usually means going to a quiet place. But this isn't always feasible, we need to master the art of thinking deeply while going about our daily duties. It may seem a hard thing to do, but we do it all the time anyway, and some of us are very good at it.

We worry on the way to work, at work, and on the way back home from work, and we carry on fretting while at home doing our chores. We seem to be able to fit worrying into our daily routines with ease, and worrying is nothing but deep thought about negative things. If we can combine working with unproductive thinking, surely we can do the same with productive thinking.

Some activities require full attention and should not be done while we're deep in thought, but we can think deeply in the shower, while cooking and also at the gym. We need to be intentional about our thought life and not leave our minds unfocused. Otherwise, we'll end up getting caught up in unproductive thoughts again.

Set aside time for thinking every day, and go for walks with the sole purpose of giving yourself over to deep thought. First, though, you'll need to get rid of any worrying thoughts, and then focus your mind on the topic you want to think about. Carry on thinking about it until you've reached a conclusion. If you need to take a break, do so, but don't forget to return to that thought later.

Be persistent

Thinking is hard work, not because it's complicated but because it involves commitment. To get the results you want you must be prepared to stick at it for long periods and persevere even when there's no breakthrough in sight. You should adopt the curiosity of a child, and ask questions.

You also need to think beyond just solving problems. This is what the world's greats do. Einstein, for instance, carried on studying problems after he'd found the solutions he was after. He wasn't merely interested in solving conundrums; he was also out to learn as much as he could about them, and so his discoveries stood out as a result. That commitment—to go a step further—is what put him ahead of the pack.

Thinking is like digging a well. You may find water at 20 feet, but if you want *clean* water, you'll need to dig deeper.

How to think

There are different types of thinking, as we mentioned earlier. There's critical thinking and analytical thinking. There's also convergent thinking, divergent thinking, sequential thinking and holistic thinking. Each type serves a different purpose.

Analytical thinking

If you want to fix a faulty machine, you first need to identify the broken part. You could diagnose the fault with appropriate computer software. You could also take the machine apart and look for any faulty or broken parts, replace them, and then put the machine back together and see if it works. Alternatively, you could use the power of your imagination. If you know the workings of the broken machine, you could work out in your mind which part was probably the faulty one; open that part of the machine and fix it. That's analytical thinking.

When you see your doctor about a health problem, he or she first listens to you and then decides whether your problem requires further investigation. Doctors rely on their knowledge of diseases and of the investigations required to make a diagnosis. But they must also carefully consider and understand your complaint before proposing an investigation. This also requires analytical thinking.

Analytical thinking is what detectives use to track down the perpetrators of crimes. They try to put themselves in the perpetrator's shoes and think as they do. This enables the detectives to work out how they themselves would have acted in that situation. Analytical thinking requires the use of imagination.

Analytical thinking is used to solve puzzles, and many of the conundrums we come across daily. It accounts for a lot of the innovation we see around us. We all have this capacity, but innovators have developed theirs through frequent use, and are, as such, called geniuses.

One thing I admire about the Dutch is their mastery over water. Since most of the country lies below sea level, the threat of flooding is constant. Because they've developed such ingenious ways of dealing with the problem, the Dutch display little anxiety about flooding. They even build their houses very close to bodies of water without any worry. With a complex system of canals, locks, dams and dykes, they can afford to push boundaries and make the most of the land they have.

This kind of ingenuity comes from analytical thinking. It involves studying a problem until you've understood every aspect of it. The reason that not many of us engage in analytical thinking often is probably that this process requires patience. We try it for a while but soon give up and find someone to help us deal with our problems. If only we would persevere!

Never in the history of this planet has there been a problem that could resist the power of patient thought. We'll all find solutions to our problems if we follow Newton's approach and think about them long enough.

Critical thinking

When we engage in critical thinking, we examine the validity, authenticity or accuracy of an argument, a position or a conclusion. If someone tells you that it's about to rain, the first thing you do is look at the sky. If you see dark clouds gathering, then you know it must be true, but if the sky is blue and the sun is shining, then you begin to doubt their claim. That's an example of critical thinking.

Critical thinking involves the use of logic, and it helps us to determine if something is true or makes sense. When we engage in critical thinking, we don't accept things at face value; we ask questions and challenge assumptions. When someone says: "that doesn't make sense" or "it sounds too good to be true", it 's an indication that they've been thinking critically about the issue in question.

Critical thinking is a defence against deception, and indeed against self-deception. We're less likely to fall victim to a scam when we ask probing questions. Equally, we can reduce the incidence of mistakes and false starts by questioning our own thinking. Critical thinking is all about asking questions, and the most important ones start with; what, how and why. If someone comes to you with a proposal, you should first ask: "What's this all about?"

Let them describe it in detail and in their own words. When they're through, start asking *how* questions. Go into as much technical detail as you can, and find out how the proposal would work. Look for any inconsistencies in what they say.

Finally, ask *why* questions. The proposal may seem workable, but you need to know what's in it for you and for the person suggesting it. Follow these steps, and you'll save yourself a lot of hassle.

Divergent versus convergent thinking

If I asked you to name the country with the largest population in the world, the answer would be very specific. You'd reach for information already stored in your memory, and if it wasn't there, you'd attempt to work it out. With a general knowledge of geography, you could arrive at the right answer by way of elimination. This process would involve convergent thinking. This kind of thinking involves counting things in and ruling other things out. It requires the use of the imagination as well as some knowledge of the subject. Convergent thinking requires logic and high levels of concentration.

On the other hand, if I asked you to name ten uses of a spoon, and you only knew three, you could not rely solely on the information you already had. You'd need to create new information as it were. You'd need to think about a spoon in ways you hadn't done before. You'd consider its shape, the material it's made of and be as imaginative as you could. This is divergent thinking.

When we improvise, we're engaging in divergent thinking. When we're in a new situation and have to deal with new situations, divergent thinking kicks into action.

Divergent thinking requires a break with convention. In the above example, thinking about a spoon only in relation to cooking and dining would restrict your imagination, making it harder to come up with new ideas. To be really inventive you need to push the boat out, and leave behind familiar trails. This requires a measure of adventurousness.

We use divergent thinking when we need new ideas. Corporations looking for new solutions encourage their employees to engage in divergent thinking. This brainstorming is usually done in groups and is followed by an attempt to turn the ideas generated into workable solutions.

When we get stuck in life, it's often because we've neglected to engage in divergent thinking. Many of us go through life mastering the art of convergent thinking, but don't learn to think laterally. And this is partly due to the structure of our education systems. Except for a few subjects, formal education consists primarily of activities designed to teach the skill of recognising the familiar. We're fed information, and then that information is elicited in the exams we sit. Our exams consist of multiple-choice questions, so we end up perfecting the art of finding the single best option, and we become experts at ruling things out.

This is all, of course, an unavoidable part of learning, but the end result conditions us to expect a range of solutions to choose from when we have a problem. Our lives revolve around spotting the familiar, and the things that come along with it, so we're merely sticking with what we know. Stepping off the well-marked trail is, for many of us, a big challenge. Hence, when facing a problem for which there are no right or wrong answers, and with no range of solutions to choose from, we feel lost.

I see this difficulty with university students all the time. Unless they've been studying a professional course with a predetermined career pathway, they're often at a loss to know what to do once they graduate. Having spent so much time in the education system, they've majored in convergent thinking and neglected divergent thinking.

Restricted imaginations

If I asked you to name a footballer, your mind would probably gravitate to names such as Cristiano Ronaldo, Lionel Messi, Luka Modric, or Eden Hazard. Do you know why? These are well-known. They're often in the news, so we often hear about them. And because we hear about them, we also think about them, maybe without even realising it. You might be aware of many other footballers, but their names wouldn't come to mind immediately because you haven't been thinking about them.

The implication here is that our routines and lifestyles can affect our capacity to think creatively. If we watch the same kind of TV shows, interact with the same people, visit the same or similar holiday destinations year in, year out, and never try anything new, we end up getting caught up in an information loop. This situation makes it hard to think creatively. When faced with a challenge we'll find ourselves reaching for the information we're most frequently exposed to. This may then lead to uninspiring choices or an inability to solve problems. To kickstart creative thinking, we need to shake up our habits, try new things, and meet new people.

Divergent thinking doesn't come naturally

This *name a footballer* task is supposed to trigger divergent thinking, and yet for many of us, it most certainly won't. Unless you're told specifically to do so, you're unlikely to stretch your imagination and come up with an obscure answer. Likewise, in naming ten uses of a spoon, you would only start thinking outside the box when you'd run out of options. In other words, divergent thinking doesn't come naturally. When faced with a problem, we all reach for the solutions we're already familiar with or the ones that seem to thrust themselves upon us. But the danger is that those may not be the best ones, and by reaching for those solutions we risk filling our lives with the same mediocre choices.

If we want to make the most of our lives, we need to make a conscious effort to ignore the obvious choices that thrust themselves upon us. We need to be more adventurous and wander off the well-trodden paths. Only then can we make truly exciting discoveries. Otherwise, we'll fill our lives with predictable choices and missed opportunities.

Another thing to note about divergent thinking is that it cannot be done under pressure. When under pressure, we always go for the obvious, because it's the simpler option. You might know of many other footballers, but their names won't come to mind immediately if you're put on the spot.

When to do what

We need to use divergent thinking when facing a career choice, for example, or looking for a job, but many of us engage in convergent thinking instead. We try to choose from a range of options and tailor our job searches to match our qualifications. If we studied physics, then we look for teaching jobs. If we studied law, we apply to a law firm. But instead of going for the obvious, we ought to be asking ourselves what we want from life.

To think creatively is to think broadly. As a medical student, you need to ask yourself which health problem you want to solve, rather than which field of medicine you wish to specialise in. Don't just aim to be a doctor, strive to become a healthcare provider. This will broaden your horizons. Take the limits off your imagination and think like a child. Think about what you could become if time and money weren't an issue. That's how to make the most of your life.

Don't try them together

Have you ever been to a meeting that ended without anything being agreed, or to a brainstorming session that concluded without any concrete ideas being put forward? Here's what probably happened: you all attempted divergent and convergent thinking at the same time. Some people suggested new ideas, others pointed out immediately why those ideas wouldn't work, and the rest kept their mouths shut for fear of looking stupid. In the end, nothing could be agreed.

The truth is that divergent and convergent thinking cannot be practised at the same time because they cancel each other out. This is as true of individuals than it is of groups. You cannot generate ideas and evaluate them at the same time. Doing that means shutting off the creative side of your mind and limiting idea generation. But if you set your mind free from this limitation, you'll be able to think more creatively and generate ideas more easily.

Convergent thinking requires critical thinking, thereby placing a limitation on your ability to think creatively. It's like having a critical person in your mind telling you that your ideas won't work. So, do your brainstorming first, and then try to find a way to turn your ideas into workable solutions. Only when you've generated enough ideas should you consider the merits of each. Allow your mind to roam freely while you're brainstorming.

How to kickstart your thought life

- Take time to study your problems—don't rush into solving them.
- Don't assume there's a single solution to a problem.
- When searching for a solution to a difficult problem, you'll find it helps to break it down into parts; then study each part carefully.
- When making a choice, don't go for the first thing that comes to mind. Consider all the options carefully. Weigh up the merits of each option before making a decision.
- Most thinking is done to answer a question—the broader the question, the more of the mind it opens up. Therefore, don't ask what car you should buy. Ask instead what means of transport you need. Don't ask what you can do with your qualifications. Ask what you want from life. And then get the necessary qualifications to make it happen.
- There are many obstacles to creative thinking, and fear is one of them. The fear of the unknown, and of making a mistake can put shackles on the imagination and hinder creativity. If you've been living in fear, then this is probably why you're struggling to

create the future you desire. Get rid of your anxieties, and you'll be able to think freely and generate new ideas.

- Be willing to step into the unknown. Sir Isaac Newton once said: "Every great discovery begins with a bold guess." To make the most of your life, you'll need to stretch your imagination and do something you haven't done before. This requires new thinking. You must be ready to climb over barriers and venture into the no-go areas in your mind. Doubtless, you'll make mistakes, but you might discover something special—your discovery might pave the way for others to make even more significant discoveries. So, don't be afraid to think beyond your comfort zone. Follow your hunch, think laterally, and let your imagination loose!

- Be curious—chase after any idea you find fascinating. Many great discoveries were made this way.

- Question everything, and don't take anything for granted. Don't accept things at face value.

- Routines are very helpful—these help us to structure our day. When you have a routine, you waste little time wondering what to do, and it's also easier to overcome your lack of motivation then. But routines can become habits, and habits lead to repetitive thought patterns, which make it harder to solve problems. For this reason, many of us are stuck where we are in life—our routines have boxed us in, and we can only think along familiar lines. To get around this problem, we need to shake up our routines every now and again. This will liberate the mind from the dreary familiarity of our everyday lives and expose it to new information.

- Being in a new environment often makes us more willing to try new things. We often switch on the slightly more boisterous version of ourselves and cast off restraint, especially if no one in the new environment knows us. Sometimes this gets us into trouble, but that needn't be the case. We can capitalise on the freedom we experience in a new environment and dare to think thoughts we're often too scared to entertain in our usual environments. Consider your holidays an opportunity, not only for relaxing and renewing your strength, but also to kickstart new thinking.

- Make every effort to meet new people and learn from them. When on holiday, make an effort to interact with the people you come across, especially the locals. See how they live, and you'll gain new perspectives on your life. Don't limit yourself to just having fun—let your holidays enrich your mind and enhance your thinking!

- Beware of rules, conventions, expectations and traditions. Rules affect the way we think and act. They create no-go areas in our minds and restrict the mental space in which we operate.

- When you start a new job and learn new rules, you end up internalising them. You tell yourself that the only way to avoid violating those rules is to stop thinking about the things they forbid. And if you're a very anxious person, you might even create additional rules for yourself that will enable you to adhere to the procedures at the workplace. Add to this your daily routines, and you'll end up with a very limited imagination, making it hard to think outside the box.

- Soldiers, doctors, and to some degree other healthcare professionals, all endure more restrictions at work than the average employee, and they all tend to think along similar lines. I've seen members of the same profession struggle with a problem, the solution to which seemed obvious to people from a completely different background. The only way to explain this seemed to be that the restrictions they endured at work were having a limiting effect on their thinking.

- You need to be aware of this if you belong to a highly regulated profession, and make a conscious effort to stretch your imagination. Mix with people from other professional backgrounds, especially, when facing an important decision. Sample their views, and you'll be amazed at how different their perspective is from yours. You'll also have a better chance of reaching a more balanced decision.

- To think is to ask questions. But you can only ask meaningful questions if you know something about the subject you're addressing. Many professional people restrict their learning to topics related to their work, and occasionally, their hobbies; but to make the most of our lives, we need to read more widely to widen and enhance our thinking.

- A lot of the thinking we do every day is repetitive and unproductive. We dwell on past mistakes and the hurtful things that people have said to us. We go over the same issues again and again without coming to any meaningful conclusions, and some of us are at our creative best when brooding over these unhelpful thoughts. Yet, we seem to draw a blank when it comes to problem-solving.

- One way of getting around this is to record your thoughts. If you catch yourself ruminating, grab your smartphone, hit record, think aloud and watch your thoughts change. Ruminating is often an attempt to process unacceptable feelings and emotions, but there's often very little logic involved because most of it is unconscious. When you record your thoughts, you bring them out into the open as it were. Your thoughts change from unconscious to conscious, which makes it easier to question them.

- This is the very principle on which certain forms of psychotherapy are based. Therapists help clients to uncover unhelpful thought patterns and challenge them. But who says you can't do this yourself? So next time you catch yourself thinking unhelpful thoughts grab your smartphone and hit record and watch your thought processes change.

Key facts:

- Constructive thinking requires time and patience
- Everyone can engage in goal-directed thinking
- Goal-directed thinking leads to solutions
- If we want to lead productive lives, we must be intentional about our thought life
- No problem can resist the power of thought

- Critical thinking is about asking questions, and the important ones start with what, how and why
- Critical thinking places thoughts and actions under scrutiny; it helps to challenge assumptions
- Critical thinking protects us from deception and from building our lives on assumptions
- Analytical thinking involves breaking down problems and looking for patterns; it also helps us to understand our problems, which makes it easier to solve them
- Divergent thinking helps us to generate new ideas, and it promotes creativity, helping us to solve problems when there are no ready-made solutions
- Convergent thinking helps to solve problems when we know the kind of answer we're looking for

Some points to consider:

- How do you use your mental faculties? Do you think more or worry more?
- When last did you solve a problem through thinking?
- How do you spend your downtime? Do you think? What about?
- How can you improve your thinking ability?

Chapter 11

Everyone's got talent

Talent, according to the Macmillan dictionary, is the "natural ability for being good at a particular activity". Note how the definition refers to being *good* at something, but doesn't say you have to be exceptionally good or outstanding to be called talented. Yet, that's not how many of us see it. We often think of talent as something that draws applause. We don't understand that talent only draws applause when it's been developed.

Most of us would be impressed if we heard a three-year-old play a simple tune like Little Bird on the piano. And that's because it's an exceptional thing for a child of that age to do. However, if that same child, now an adult in their 30s played the tune, we might not take any notice. Why? Because it's easy for an adult to learn that tune.

Moreover, we'd expect that the talent we saw the child display earlier to have evolved into a more refined skill. That, of course, requires hard work. The truth is, what most people call talent is nothing but a product of hard graft. Indeed, people are called "talented" not because they were born with a natural ability but because they've worked hard to develop a skill.

Take footballers for example; many of them learned to play football and then turned it into a career. Today, they're called talented. Some of them weren't good at dribbling, to begin with, but they learnt it. Maybe they're still not brilliant at manoeuvring the ball, but they've found a position on the pitch that best suits their abilities, and where dribbling isn't needed as much.

Didier Drogba may not have been the best dribbler in the world during his playing career, but that didn't stop him from becoming one of the most revered strikers in the history of the English Premiership, and a household name among football fans the world over. His tall stature and athletic build gave him the edge over his opponents, and he used it in aerial duels beating them to the ball time and again. His strength, speed and agility more than compensated for his average dribbling skills, and he managed to score goals even when the odds were stacked up against him.

What I'm saying is that you may not be super-talented in the conventional sense of the word, but nature has given you a head start in some aspect of life, and it's your job to discover your natural ability and develop it. You'll then need to find the best platform for showcasing it. You won't excel at everything, no matter how hard you try, but if you commit to improving yourself in those areas you're already good at, you'll be off to a flying start.

Talent is any skill you're prepared to develop.

Everyone is talented

You may think that you have no talents at all, but don't be in such a hurry to write yourself off. To be gifted is to be naturally good at something, but you won't know that unless you give it a try. You'll never know that you have a flair for writing poetry unless you try it. Neither will you know about your manoeuvring ability unless you learn how to drive. You won't discover your leadership skills until you get the opportunity to lead others. Tiger Woods wouldn't have found his talent if he hadn't tried his hands at golf. So, before you conclude that you have no natural abilities, perhaps you ought to get out there and try something new. No one came to this world empty-handed, and that includes you. We all have something to offer.

Focus on what you have

Nicholas James Vujicic, pastor and motivational speaker, was born with Tetra-Amelia syndrome. The condition left him without arms or legs, but that didn't stop him from developing what nature had given him. Today he's a source of inspiration to many across the world. How did he do it? By focusing on what he had rather than on what he didn't have. We all have something to offer, and if we stop complaining about our limitations, and arm ourselves with a positive mindset instead, we'll soon discover where our advantage lies.

Don't neglect that gift!

Imagine that you are a witness to a gruesome road accident. As you watch from the other side of the road, you see a crowd gathering at the scene. No one does anything at first, but then a man soon steps out, approaches the apparently lifeless body of one of the victims and attempts first aid. You feel alarmed when you see he doesn't know what he's doing. You've been trained in CPR (first aid for someone who is unconscious and not breathing), and you think you can do a better job than him. You want to help, but before you step out, a thought crosses your mind: what if you get it wrong? What if you make an absolute fool of yourself? At this point, your desire to help seeps out of your body.

While you're still standing there contemplating your next move, an ambulance arrives, and the crew takes over. You breathe a sigh of relief. You didn't have to intervene. But why didn't you act? There can only be one answer: you lacked self-belief. If you believed in your abilities enough, you'd have stepped out and helped. One of the reasons we step aside for someone else to take charge when we know that we're better placed to address a situation is that we don't fully believe in our abilities.

But there's an even more fundamental issue here: someone's life was at stake, but you let your hang-ups get in the way. What if the accident victim had been your mother or daughter, a friend or someone else you loved? Would you have been so concerned about making a fool of yourself? Would you have hesitated? Probably not! You'd have felt a greater sense of urgency that may have spurred you on to act.

One of the reasons we neglect to put our talents to use is that we don't understand the loss that results, not only to ourselves, but also to others. We don't appreciate that we are often the key to easing someone else's pain, or that our own happiness is often tied to the development of our abilities.

The natural abilities given to you allow you to have a head start in life, and the good news is you can put them to use even if you have a disability; so why waste them?

Your talents can catapult you to greatness, and like dreams; they are an expression of the soul. People get to see more of your personality when you develop and then showcase your abilities. This is why you cannot make the development of your talents optional. Don't treat your gift as a dispensable accessory. Don't get so caught up in the rat race that you forget to nurture what nature gave you. Develop it, and you'll grow an inch taller; not literally, of course.

Don't be scared to be unique

Our talents make us unique, but uniqueness is something many of us struggle with. We want to blend in and be like everyone else. But if nature wanted us all to be the same, it would have made us that way. We're all different for a reason, so don't despise your uniqueness.

Where are my talents?

Many of our talents are hidden in the things we do daily. Our body features also point to our hidden abilities. Earlier, when we were discussing the human body, we saw how the whole body is neatly fitted together. But this perfection isn't limited to the body—it's manifested in our entire being.

Your natural abilities probably match your physical attributes. Together, they make you a winner, and if you discover and nurture those abilities, you'll be off to a flying start. So don't despise your physical attributes. Don't hate your body because you don't look like everyone else because your physical characteristics may be an indication of an unusual talent.

Take stock

The easiest way to identify your talents is to do an inventory. Ask yourself these questions:

- What am I good at?
- What do I get complimented on?

- What do I enjoy doing?
- Which activities or tasks come easily?

Make time to think about these questions, and continue thinking about them while going about your daily activities. Think about them while you're eating, when you're lying in bed unable to sleep or while out for a walk etc. If an idea comes to mind, note it down.

A lot of talent gets displayed in the things we do every day, both at work and outside it. You'll learn a great deal by alloting two days, one a workday and the other at the weekend, to note down all the tasks you perform, and all the activities you get involved in. Do this for the entire day, from morning to night.

At work, note down such activities as attending and chairing meetings, supervising employees, and working in customer service. At the weekend, record your household chores and make a note of the things you enjoy doing. A lot of talent gets displayed when we're having fun or doing something we love. Therefore think about social events and leisure activities as areas where you might be demonstrating some of your natural abilities.

The next thing to do is to identify the skills and attributes required for each task on your list. But to do so, you first need to break down each task into smaller components. In some jobs, this is a fairly easy thing to do. Someone working as an auxiliary nurse or a support worker in a nursing home has to perform a range of simple tasks such as feeding the clients, cleaning, bathing and maintaining personal hygiene, administering medication, coordinating leisure activities, one to one time with clients or accompanying clients to appointments. Each of these activities requires different skills and attributes. While the tasks themselves may be quite simple and can be learned easily, they require a lot of patience, which is not something that everyone has. Patience, therefore, needs to be listed among the attributes needed for this kind of job. Being a support worker also exposes you to teamwork, and allows you to develop flexibility and versatility through the varied nature of the tasks you perform in each shift.

A hotel manager has to ensure the smooth running of the hotel, and customer satisfaction is the top priority. To achieve this goal, he or she must provide training and supervision for the other members of staff, as well as keep them motivated. He or she also needs to coordinate staff rotas and monitor the quality of service delivered by each worker. This requires people skills and attention to detail. This manager must also be perceptive and dutiful and possess organisational skills. These skills and attributes are all transferable and can, therefore, be listed on the manager's CV to make their next job application more effective.

Completing an inventory of your skills can also help with career progression. You'll be better placed to consciously develop your skills when you know which ones you already possess. You can also work hard to acquire new skills to complement those you already have.

This approach can help determine if you're suited to a different career. First, you should identify the skills needed in that occupation, and you can do so by establishing the tasks that need to be performed in that type of work. This should make it easier to know which skills you have, and which ones you'd need to acquire.

Stand-up comedians, for instance, need to be able to speak in front of a crowd and tell a story in a way that holds their audiences spellbound. They also need to be able to act, as some scenes have to be acted out, and they must be alert to spot behaviours that can be incorporated into their jokes. Having a natural ability to perform these tasks helps, but such skills can also be learned. It may come as a surprise to know that not every stand-up comedian was born with an innate ability to hold audiences spellbound for 2 hours. Some were once terrified of crowds, but have mastered the art of public speaking and are now good on-stage entertainers. These things can be learned, you know.

You need a mirror

The easiest way to find out what you're good at is to ask someone who knows you well. As we interact with people, our abilities, skills and personal attributes impress upon them, and they form opinions about our strengths. Sometimes they compliment us directly, at other times they drop hints in non-verbal reactions, although I would be careful with interpreting these as one can easily get it wrong. It's always better to ask, but before you do, prepare a list of things you regularly do. Then ask someone you trust to comment on your ability to perform each task on your list. Let them rate your skills on a scale of one to five, one being poor and five being very good. Ask why they think you're good at each task.

You need exposure

When I was in primary school, I knew I wasn't good at football (soccer), and since it was the only sport available, it seemed that I wasn't good at sporting activities in general. All that changed when I was exposed to basketball in secondary school. I found out that I could do with my hands what I couldn't do with my legs, and so I made it into my house team.

I remember asking to be subbed during an inter-house match. I was exhausted having not done much training.

"Do you want us to lose this match?" quipped the team captain.

That was the first time anyone had ever complimented me on my sporting ability, and it had happened because I was exposed to something new. So, get out there and try new things so you can discover what *you're* naturally good at!

Turn your know-how into mojo

Some of us know we have talents but lack confidence in our abilities, and that's because we lack belief. Knowledge and belief aren't the same things. Knowing something doesn't always lead to action, whereas believing does. If someone told you there was gold buried in your garden and you believed them, you'd probably take time off work, set up a tent in your backyard, get some tools and start digging. You wouldn't ignore that piece of information if you truly believed it because belief leads to action.

Likewise, if someone told you that the building you were in was on fire, and you believed them, you'd get out. Belief leads to action. The reason you haven't done anything with your talents yet is due to a lack of belief. You know about your innate qualities, but you don't believe they could amount to anything. That's why you've chosen instead to learn a different skill in order to earn a living while ignoring what nature gave you. When you start believing in your natural abilities, you'll also commit to turning them into products and services that will benefit you and the world at large. Thankfully, there's a way to turn your knowledge into belief.

When we're exposed to something for a long time, we start to believe it. The cultural beliefs that we hold onto rigidly aren't necessarily evidence-based or a product of careful analysis, but merely ideas that were handed down to us by tradition, and which we, through continual exposure, have come to accept as facts. Today, these beliefs form part of our wider belief systems and dictate our actions. We resent it if we're challenged or questioned about them.

Many of us have also been exposed to unhelpful comments and criticisms for a long time. Some of us have been told that we'd never amount to anything, and sadly, we've believed it. That piece of information, now one of our core beliefs, is hindering our progress. And yet, it is most certainly untrue. The good news is that we can now employ the same process that led to the formation of this unhelpful belief, but this time in our favour. We can start telling ourselves the things we're good at. If we do this long enough, we'll form new opinions about ourselves.

The mind will believe anything as long as it's exposed to it for long enough, and there is no evidence to the contrary. Therefore, feed on the information in your inventory. Read it every day and add in any helpful new facts you discover about yourself. Construct a few meaningful quotes about your skills and attributes, note them down, and place them in different places around your house so that you'll come across them as you go about your daily routine. Make an audio recording of these quotes, and listen to it on your way to work, while you're out on a walk and while lying in bed unable to sleep. Do this over and over again and watch your belief system change.

Action required

A change of belief is never complete without corresponding action. Faith without works is dead. Unless you start acting on your new beliefs, they'll soon be overthrown by the negative opinions you hold about yourself. And those remain entrenched because you've acted on them repeatedly.

Therefore, start acting on your new beliefs. Start writing that book, start playing that sport, start offering your services to people, start doing the things you know you're good at. Provide your mind with the evidence it needs to consolidate the knowledge about your abilities into a belief system. And while you're at it, why not go a step further and try your hands at the things you think you aren't much good at? You'll find that to be even more liberating!

Key facts:

- Everyone has talents
- Talent isn't necessarily what draws applause, but any skill that you're prepared to develop
- The key to becoming successful is discovering what you have, not what you don't have
- Talents are moulded through hard work
- Your skills are hidden in your day-to-day activities
- Your natural abilities are hidden in your physical attributes and in your personality
- To develop your latent abilities, you first need to discover them
- You must have confidence in your abilities in order to improve them
- You can turn knowledge about your talents into confidence in your ability

Chapter 12

Let it shine

In this chapter, we'll discuss how to develop your talent. The only way to grow your talent is in fact to use it. Talent is like muscle, it improves with use, and the key to developing it is to use it for other people's benefit rather than your own.

If you're a musician, you need to let someone else enjoy your music, as only then will you get the feedback you need to help you improve. If you're your own audience, then your own impressions are likely to be skewed; you might be too self-critical or ignore obvious mistakes.

When I learnt to play the guitar, I did most of it on my own, and in the process, I picked up a few bad habits that made it harder for me to develop my skill any further. That happened because there was no one to point out my mistakes. That's why you need someone to observe so they can give you valuable feedback.

By performing in front of an audience—no matter how small (even one person is enough)—you're developing not only your technical skill but also your performance ability. The two are definitely not the same: you may be good at playing in private, but struggle to deliver the same quality in public, so that's another reason to perform in front of other people.

The challenges of self-expression

The main challenge of performing in front of an audience is that if someone doesn't like it, they might not mind letting you know. Some people are so blunt with their feedback that you almost need therapy

119

after colliding with their opinions. This can make you a little unsure about giving any future performances.

Singers are more likely to experience this than anyone else. By its nature, singing attracts feedback, and most people feel compelled to comment when they hear someone sing. Perhaps this is because singing stirs up emotions, and giving feedback is, to some extent, an emotional affair. Your music video on YouTube is likely to attract comments, and who's to say whether they'll all be positive. Negative responses can be hard to take and can make you a little hesitant about uploading any more videos on the internet.

One of the reasons we struggle with feedback is that we approach it on an all-or-nothing basis. We put our performances out there and expect only one type of response—an overwhelmingly positive one. And if we receive even one critical comment, we conclude that we must have performed badly. This all-or-nothing approach equates ovation with approbation and lack of applause with disapproval, when life is, in fact, far more complex than that.

As children, we were praised for our smallest achievements, but as we grow older, the praise thins out, and unless we've done something exceptional, only our most ardent admirers will acknowledge our accomplishments. Some will actually find it easier to criticise us than show approval, especially those with little or no emotional connection to us. An absence of applause does not, therefore, mean it's a flop. It may be only an indication that we haven't put out an outstanding performance, but that's nothing to be ashamed of. After all, we haven't come up with the finished article yet.

We must also remember that reactions to our products or performances depend on many factors that do not all relate to the quality of the product or the performance itself. If your act follows an outstanding one in a comedy show, for example, it may come across as average even though it might have been quite good.

Moreover, feedback is nothing but the expression of an opinion, and opinions, as the saying goes, are like noses, everyone has one, and it usually has a couple of holes in it. In other words, everyone is entitled to an opinion, but that doesn't mean necessarily that those views are accurate. They're shaped by past experiences. If someone rates your product or service as good or bad, they're essentially comparing it with other products or services they've seen or used. They may not have seen every single product out there, so their feedback needs to be put into perspective.

Finally, some people offer an opinion, not because they have one to give, but because they've been asked for one. If you walk up to someone and ask: "How did you find my performance?" They'll feel obliged to say something, but they may not have had time to reflect, so their words may not represent their true opinions.

When it all goes quiet

Negative feedback can be hard to take, and the lack of feedback, which is more common, can be a challenge too. The worst thing about it is that it leaves you wondering whether or not your performance or product was liked. In that moment of uncertainty, you may turn against yourself. Some of us are our own worst critics, and even when we're not criticised, we end up criticising ourselves. This habit then robs us of confidence.

But, as mentioned earlier, giving feedback is an emotional affair. A performance that stirs up emotions will get louder applause than one that doesn't, even though the latter might have been technically superior. This is why photos and funny videos get more *likes* on social media than educational ones.

How to handle feedback

Keeping the above points in mind, one needs to have a systematic approach to feedback, and it's important to have the right mindset. Here are a few tips that could make the process easier:

- Have reasonable expectations of yourself and your performance. Don't treat your performance like a "great unveiling" or you'll also expect a round of applause, which might not materialise. Instead, regard it as an opportunity for further development. Remember that this is not the finished article.

- Keep your feelings out of the process, and treat feedback as you would any piece of technical information.
- Take every piece of feedback with a pinch of salt. Opinions aren't necessarily factual, but they may contain a grain of truth. Focus on the truth and leave the rest. If you're struggling with this, then ask for help.
- Don't attach importance to any comments just because of the standing of the person giving it. Evaluate each piece of feedback on its own merits; accepting or rejecting it accordingly. If you struggle with this, ask for help.
- People who give feedback also like to get a response. They like to know whether or not their comments were helpful. Let's say that you've uploaded your music, artwork or some other creative piece onto the internet, and someone has made an unhelpful remark in the comments section. This might leave you feeling discouraged or defensive, but you could also choose a very different response.

    You could thank the author of that comment for taking the time to give feedback. That alone might help settle some of the negative feelings you might have had.

    You could then go on to ask them to give more constructive criticism of your performance. People often leave comments, especially negative ones, in the heat of the moment without thinking through their responses. By posing this question, you're giving them a chance to reflect. This might result in a more constructive response. But if their next comment is equally emotional, thank them as before, and explain how vital it is that they offer more concrete feedback. By doing this, you're teaching yourself to contain the negative emotions that critical feedback often evokes, and you're also helping to educate someone on giving constructive feedback. Repeat it a few times, and you'll lose your fear of negative appraisal, and those who read your friendly exchange with this person will learn a thing or two about giving feedback.
- Timing is everything, especially on social media. If you post something in the morning when most people are getting ready

for work or taking their children to school, it may not get much attention. Some people check their social media feeds when they arrive at work but usually do so very quickly, so they may not read your post. And if they do read it, they may not have time to comment. By lunchtime, your post will have been crowded out by other posts. This is how things get missed.

In other words, not getting any *likes* on your video post does not necessarily equate to a lack of appreciation. If you post something and don't receive any *likes*, find out why you didn't. Post the same material at a different time and compare the responses.

- Familiarity with the audience counts an awful lot on social media. People are kinder to artists they already know and love, which is why it's essential to generate followers through a range of activities that give you a continuous presence on the platform you're using. By doing this, you'll increase the chances of views and responses for your posts.

- We all like the warm fuzzy feeling that comes with being appreciated. But it's also ok when we're not applauded because this helps to keep us grounded, especially if we're getting carried away with our successes. A lack of applause can also provide the motivation we need to keep improving ourselves.

- You can learn to attract feedback—you'll find a few YouTube videos that teach this. For online content, clear labelling helps. If you give your post the wrong title, no one will take much notice, and you won't get much feedback. Videos with eye-catching thumbnails are a lot more likely to get plenty of views. Before posting material on a Whatsapp or Facebook group, see the current topic and judge the mood before you do so. Don't publish your post in the middle of a heated discussion about something else, or it'll go unnoticed. Weekends and evenings are good times to post material on WhatsApp and Facebook groups. People are more likely to check their social media feeds at those times, and they're also more likely to leave comments.

- Momentum is everything on social media. If you're constantly posting interesting material, your followers will see you as their *go-to* place for entertainment. They'll wait for your posts and react to them. If you're inconsistent in the regularity your posts, you won't get as many *likes*. So, don't keep your fans waiting for too long or else they'll lose patience and go somewhere else.

Managing positive feedback

We all need as much encouragement as we can get to help us in our development. But sometimes, positive comments can be just as unsettling as negative ones. They can send your emotions sky-high, but then a single negative response can bring them crashing down. Besides, you can get carried away with too many compliments, and start thinking more of yourself than you ought to. You may then, perhaps unwittingly, let the quality of your performances or products start to drop.

Yes, it's good to delight in positive feedback, but you can go a step further and harness its power. Try to find out why someone liked your performance or product, and use that information to help yourself improve. Always show appreciation for the comments you receive, and then find out what aspect of the performance or product was most desirable and what could be done to make it better.

Discover your platform

Three things are required to fulfil your assignment: the person, the licence and the platform.

The person refers to your personal attributes including your physical features, your intellect and your personality traits. The licence represents the knowledge, skills and qualifications required for your assignment, and the platform is the environment, situation or setting that enables you to showcase your knowledge and skills, and helps to maximise your potential.

Platforms are about elevation; they help you to get noticed, sometimes literally. In the entertainment sector, the audience can only see the performing artists if they stand on a platform. But in a broader sense, the theatre itself is a platform because it helps the artists showcase their abilities. For a blogger, the internet is the platform, and a record label is a platform for a recording artist.

Platforms also help to maximise potential. As we explained earlier, playing as a striker best suited Didier Drogba, and this enabled him to maximise his potential. At the same time, though, he also needed to find the right club and a coach who knew how to bring out the best in him. This is something many footballers don't seem to take into account when looking for a club. Many go for the highest bidder and, in some cases, are swayed by the profile of the club; but every talent needs a platform to develop on, and the flashiest aren't necessarily the most suitable. Chelsea FC proved to be the perfect platform for Didier Drogba, and in Jose Mourinho, he found a coach who understood his unique capabilities and orchestrated a system of play to harness them. Had the player gone to a different club, he might never have become the football colossus he's turned out to be.

As a footballer, you should choose the club where you'll best fit in. You should also take into account the situation of the current coach or manager, whether they're going to be there for a long time or are likely to be replaced soon. Choose the wrong club, and you could end up halting your development.

Making the most of your platform

As you develop your potential, and your qualities begin to show, the world will start to take notice. At this point, you'll find that more opportunities open up to showcase what you have. The better you are at what you do, the more chances you'll have. Eventually, you'll be propelled onto a pedestal. This will happen when the world is persuaded that you have something special to offer. Everyone else will then shut up, and you'll be handed the microphone as you take centre stage.

In other words, your platform will grow as you get better at what you do. In the beginning, only a handful of people may be interested in what you have to offer, but the word will get around if you persevere, and you'll soon see the numbers grow.

As your popularity increases, so must the quality of your performances. You mustn't forget that the reason you're on the platform is, among other things, to develop yourself. If you lose sight of this fact and let the quality drop, you could find yourself quickly fading from the scene. This is something to bear in mind especially if you're a sportsperson or an entertainer. You mustn't get carried away with your success, and never drop your guard.

Always bear in mind your that popularity stems primarily from what you bring to the table. You may be the most likeable person on earth and have millions of fans around the world, but your fans are more interested in what you do than in who you are, and unless you maintain high standards and keep your competitive edge, you'll lose the right to be on the platform. Your fans will begin to vote with their feet. This is true of products and services as well. Maintaining high standards keeps you in the minds of your clients.

Popularity brings with it opportunities, but not all of them are worth pursuing. Some "opportunities" can actually turn out to be traps. The wrong endorsement deal can, for instance, alter your public image in ways you might not have anticipated. Equally, collaborating with the wrong artist can lose you fans. Artists hire good agents not only to represent them but also to help them make the right choices. A good agent will help you seize opportunities and avoid traps.

Be mindful of the limitations

Every platform comes with restrictions. You can only exhibit your talent to the degree to which the platform lets you. A singer is limited by the record label they have a contract with, and an actor is limited to the type of shows that the theatre they work for specialises in. You may have a broad spectrum of skills, but if you've signed a contract with a theatre that specialises in classics, you'll not get the chance to put all your skills on display. This is true of every platform; including your job because that is a kind of platform too. The workplace offers opportunities to showcase your skills and talents, but there are often many restrictions. If you work on a factory floor, then your individuality is not needed. Indeed, it could be seen as a hindrance. Factories are designed to run smoothly, and that requires every activity to be scripted and choreographed. You may have organisational skills but you won't have many opportunities to put them to use if all your employer wants is for you to press a button or move an item onto a conveyor belt.

It's the same with training and development. Your employer may offer courses, but these will be dictated by the needs of the organisation rather than your own. You may wish to develop leadership skills, but if you're not in a management position, then your employer might not deem it necessary to send you on leadership courses. It is therefore up to you to seek out opportunities for your development and put to use those talents that aren't required at work.

Key facts:

- To develop your talent, you need feedback
- People who give feedback also need feedback
- Lack of feedback does not necessarily mean the performance, product or service is poor
- You're not the finished article yet, so it's ok if you get negative feedback
- You need a platform on which to demonstrate your talent
- Platforms help you to get noticed
- Popularity needs to be managed
- Failure to manage your popularity may result in you losing it
- Your job is a platform
- Every platform comes with limitations

Chapter 13

Let your talent lead the way

Your talent is your gift to the world

Every living thing has something for its own use and something to offer to the world. A tree has roots for drawing water and nutrients from the soil, a stem for holding itself upright, and leaves for turning solar energy into food. All of the above are of direct benefit to the tree. A tree also produces fruit, which contains seeds for reproduction, but the lovely juicy pulp inside the fruit appears to bring no benefit to the tree, and yet it uses a lot of energy to produce the fruit every year. Why? Because the fruit is its gift to the world.

This principle applies to humans too. The different body parts and faculties we possess are primarily for our benefit. The eyes are for seeing, the ears are for hearing and our legs enable us to walk. These body parts bring direct benefit to us. But we also have something to offer to the world—our talent is that thing.

Our talents, interests and passions, lead to actions that bring benefits to fellow human beings and help us leave the world a better place. This is why we mustn't neglect to develop them and put them to good use. If you choose not to grow your talents, you may deprive the world of a great invention, a work of art, poem or song. The world may also miss an excellent doctor or nurse, or an amazing restaurant or hotel; so step out there and show the world what you have. Let everyone enjoy it and as they do, you will too.

Without the help of humans and animals, the fruit a tree produces will remain under the tree. But when animals eat the fruit, they excrete the seeds in their faeces. These seeds are then transported to other places. This way, the seeds are spread, and the trees can grow elsewhere. By offering something to the world for free, the tree reaps an even bigger reward—it is heir to a forest.

This is how your talent works; it's one of your most prized assets, but it will only make a way for you if you make it available to others. You could learn to play a musical instrument and enjoy playing the music alone, but that talent will only come into its own when you let others enjoy it too. People will often make a bigger deal of your abilities than you ever will, and as they do, they'll provide avenues for its development and help catapult you to greatness. Therefore, it is essential that you express your natural gifts; and even more important that you do it for the benefit of others.

All the different parts of your body and soul are for your benefit primarily, but your talent was given to you so you could put a smile on someone else's face. The paradox is that as you develop your talent and make it available to others, you benefit the most. So let your talent lead the way!

Your talent will lift you up

> *A man's gift makes room for him and brings him before great men.*

> Solomon (Proverbs 18:16 NKJV)

David was the youngest of his father's children, and the least significant. His six elder brothers were all ahead of him in the pecking order, according to the culture of Israel at that time. But David could play musical instruments, so when King Saul was ill and in distress, his servants mentioned David, whose music, they believed, would help ease the king's suffering.

Saul agreed and sent for David, and sure enough, he found relief as he listened to David playing the harp. David left the hills of Judea and went from being an insignificant shepherd boy to living in the King's palace. His gift made way for him.

While his talent was still in development, there was no way of knowing what kind of future awaited David. Likewise, you don't know where your talent will lead you. You may be a few steps away from a major breakthrough for all you know. Your talent can open doors for you, and bring you before kings and dignitaries—but only if you work hard to develop it.

Before his successes on the tennis court, British tennis ace Andy Murray was not very well-known, and few dignitaries were queuing up to see him. All that changed after he won Wimbledon. Not only was he invited to Number 10 Downing Street to meet David Cameron, the former prime minister, but he was also knighted by the Queen.

Do you remember Michael Jackson's encounter with the Sultan of Brunei? That wouldn't have happened if he hadn't developed his talent. Your talent can project you onto a platform where you'll meet world leaders. This is Bono's story. He started out as leader of the rock band, U2, but before he knew it, he was sharing a stage with world leaders seeking solutions to the world's problems. This could be your story. When you follow your talent, it takes you out on a journey of self-discovery and brings you within arm's length of your destiny.

Your talent has the potential to catapult you to greatness, but like a gem it needs polishing. People can't see the value of a diamond until it's been polished, and anyone might even tread on it, not knowing is value. Once it has been refined though, its value is revealed, and people treat it with respect. Your talent is like that, as it won't get noticed while it remains a rough gemstone—once its beauty is brought out, it will get all the attention.

Talent comes both from nature and nurture. Nature gives you the raw material, but you need to spend time improving it until you can express it well, and bring a smile to someone's face. This involves hard work, and you must be prepared to endure long periods without results. So long as you don't give up, your efforts will be rewarded.

To help you through the hard times you need to picture the end result. Read about people who have developed a similar ability. If you want to be a musician, find out how great musicians hone their skills. Read about Mozart and Beethoven as well as contemporary musicians. Be inspired by their stories, and learn from their mistakes.

Work hard to improve on what nature has given you. Make it your life's obsession to become super good at what you do. Remember that talent is of no use once you're in the grave. If you take it there without having used it here, it will have benefited no one. So get out there and develop your talent. Let your talent shine, and it will let you shine.

Case study: Anne-Marie Imafidon

It was her talent in maths and science that brought Dr Anne-Marie Imafidon into the limelight. But this is perhaps unsurprising given her pedigree: Anne-Marie comes from a family of child prodigies, and her father is a professor. By the age of 11, she had an A-level in computing, the first girl ever to do so, and at 20, she held a Master's Degree from Oxford University in Mathematics and Computer Science.

But these achievements, though impressive, could not have brought her highest recognition yet, an MBE (Member of the British Empire). When used merely for our own benefit, our talents will, at best, win us plaudits from well-wishers. But when we make them available to others, these talents can propel us to greatness, and this is true of Anne-Marie.

Anne-Marie's father, Professor Chris Imafidon a professor in Maths, did not rest on his academic laurels, but instead found a fun way to teach maths to children. And having trained his children to be child prodigies, he decided to do it for other children too.

Excellence in Education, an organisation he set up to help improve educational achievements amongst inner-city children, has helped many average children excel in their exams. Prof. Imafidon is determined to prove that, with the right approach, every child can achieve the same results that his children achieved. His message is: there's a genius in every child.

Following her father's example, Anne-Marie went down a similar route, setting up STEMettes, an award-winning social initiative aimed at encouraging girls to take up careers in science, technology, engineering and maths. Since its inception, this organisation has inspired thousands of girls across the UK, and it is for this contribution that Anne-Marie made it onto the Queen's honours list. If she'd used her talent only for her own benefit, she would not have been recognised in the same way.

Your talent is your gift to the world, and when you exercise it for that purpose, it will lift you up. It's time to discover yours and develop it; then use it for someone else's benefit. Help, support, teach, entertain, empower, and alleviate others' suffering by using the gifts that nature has given you. Let your talent lift others up, and it'll turn out to be your greatest asset.

Let your talent lift others up, and it will lift you up

You may think that Anne-Marie was destined to achieve greatness because of her background. Indeed, we could argue all day about the role her father's genes have played in her successes, but she'll be the first to tell you that what made a difference was her father's fun way of teaching. With his help, she trained herself to be a child prodigy. Do you remember what we said earlier about talent being any skill you're willing to develop? Well, it applies here.

So, if you've been wondering about your purpose and what legacy to leave behind, here's my advice: discover your natural abilities, and then start developing yourself in that area. You may never know what your life's purpose is but if you develop your talent and showcase it, you won't stray too far from that purpose. This is because your purpose is tied to your natural abilities. It's what you were built for.

Key facts:

- Your talent is your gift to the world
- Your talents can make a way for you in life and help you move from zero to hero
- Your talent is of no use when you're in the grave

Chapter 14

Make every second count

Be more frugal with your time than you are with money,
for money can be made, but you cannot make time.

They say that time is money, but I don't often come across people who give time the same respect they give money. Yet, without time none of our other resources could be put to use. You cannot fulfil your purpose without having the time to do it. This time is called *life*. Your entire life is nothing but time. If you spend an hour doing something useful, that's an hour of your life used productively. Similarly, an hour spent doing something useless is an hour lost. If you spent that time arguing with someone, you'll have lost more than an hour because you'd need more time to recover from the unfruitful thoughts and emotions the argument would have stirred up in you.

In his book, *What Do You Do With Your Time?*, Dr Sunday Adelaja writes about the three ways of passing the time. We can waste it, spend it or invest it. We waste time when we let it pass without accomplishing anything meaningful. Time is inevitably misspent when we have no clear goal or purpose.

To spend time is to engage in meaningful activity. Often, this leads to a reward. The salary we get at the end of the month is, among other things, a reward for the time and effort expended at work. This is much better than wasting time, but it's not the best use of time. The best use of time is to utilise it in an endeavour that may bring multiple returns. Time spent educating yourself is time invested because the knowledge obtained can be put to use many times over. Equally, time spent building relationships or helping people is time invested because the returns are bountiful. So be a wise time manager—*waste* no time, *spend* very little, and *invest* the rest!

The truth about time

You don't have forever

There's a cap on our lives. No one is going to live forever. If you're in the developed world, you'll probably live till you're about eighty or thereabouts. If you live in the third world though, you've got even less time to live. We've all got a limited time to do whatever we've been sent here for. We haven't got forever.

Life on earth is subject to other limitations too—and one of them is ageing. For the first twenty-something years of our lives, the body is in growth mode and grows bigger and stronger. We hit our peak in our mid-twenties or thereabouts and remain there for a while, and then it's a slow, downhill process from there. So, at forty you don't have the same resources you had when you were 20. You may be more experienced and understand the world better, but you don't have the physical prowess you once had.

As we grow older and hit our senior years, further limitations impose themselves. Our metabolism slows down, and we become a little sluggish, which restricts us yet again in what we can do. We may still be mentally sharp, but we may not be able to shuttle back and forth and crisscross the world on business trips as we did once. Unless we live with this awareness, we'll end up wasting a lot of time.

When we have something in abundance or think we do, we end up wasting some of it. It's in our nature. If you arrive at a train station and discover that your train is an hour late, you end up wasting most of that 'free time'. With time to spare, you stroll around, have a look in the shops, play games on your phone or check your news feed.

But if you suddenly discover that you'd misread the train times and that your train is about to leave, your attitude changes. You go from being relaxed to being stressed. You look for the platform the train is to depart from and make a mad dash for it.

Many of us stroll through life quite casually because we think we have lots of time to play around with, but the eighty years I mentioned earlier isn't guaranteed. No one knows how long they're going to live for, which is why we cannot afford to waste any of our time.

The only time you really have is *now*. You don't know what tomorrow will bring, so live as though today were your last day on earth. That's not to say that you should go off and blow your last penny on non-essentials; but rather that you shouldn't leave for tomorrow the things you can do today.

No extra time allowed

Life is not a football game; there is no extra time.

In a game of football (soccer) two teams play against each other for 90 minutes. If the game ends in a stalemate, they get an additional 30 minutes. But life isn't like that; you can't get any extra time. If you reach midlife and discover that you haven't achieved your goals, you can't reset the time and begin all over again.

Money can't buy you any more time

You can hire people to work for you and thereby leverage your time, but strictly speaking, you can't have more time. This makes time the most valuable resource there is. We must all learn how to manage our time wisely. We need to be more economical with our time than we are with money.

Equal distribution

Time is probably the only resource that has been equally distributed. The rich get 24 hours every day, and so do the poor. A monarch may have all the power in the world, but he cannot have a minute longer than a pauper. They both get 24 hours a day, 7 days every week and 52 weeks every year. If you feel disadvantaged in life, remember that you're on a par with the rich and powerful in this one area. This alone should put a spring in your step.

Purpose directs the use of time

While working in prisons, I discovered an astonishing truth about time. I understood how managing your time can be very hard if you don't have a purpose. Prisoners have time in abundance but very little to fill it with. That's what many of them think anyway, and they try to pass the time by using recreational drugs or taking sleeping pills. But the true reason these drugs are popular isn't a lack of activities, but a lack of purpose, as purpose directs the use of time. Those who have goals know what to do with their time. Earlier on, we mentioned how Nelson Mandela used his time in prison to develop himself. He could only do this because he had a clear goal.

Having a purpose places a demand on our time, and when we have clear goals and limited time within which to achieve them, we develop a sense of urgency. If you wake up in the morning and have a task to complete by the end of the day, you begin to experience pressure—there are only 24 hours in a day—and you'll spend some of the time doing other necessary things. If the deadline for that task is midday, you'll have an even greater sense of urgency. You must now prioritise that important task over the others. This is as true of our day-to-day activities as it is of life. If your ambition is to become a High Court judge, and you know that the average work experience needed after leaving law school is 20 years, you'll also understand that you have to start your career early. Going to law school at 50 is pointless as it will leave you no time to fulfil your ambition.

How to manage your time

Plan it

Distractions are a fact of life, and we have to tackle them. The best way to manage distractions is to plan your day, week, and indeed your month, in advance. Allocate time for everything including reading. Once you've established your schedule, you need to stick to it quite ruthlessly. Make every planned task mandatory so you'll be able to answer "no" with ease if someone asks if you're free. Don't class anything in your diary as optional; otherwise, you'll find yourself rescheduling it when something else crops up.

Let the time dedicated to an activity be proportionate to the fruitfulness of that activity and the degree to which it is related to your assignment or purpose. If it isn't related to your calling, then don't assign it too much time. Let your life goals be central to everything you do. Allocate time for the following:

Personal development

The best way to stay on top of your game is to keep improving yourself. Personal growth isn't just something to pursue in the first half of your life. You must constantly seek to improve in every area of your life by learning new things and by keeping your skills up-to-date. If you don't, you'll stagnate. Do the following regularly:

- Set aside time for reading and studying. Find out what your learning needs are and prepare a reading list. Read to enhance both your knowledge and vocabulary and also for fun. Be led by your curiosity and by the gaps in your knowledge.

  Learn to speed-read, and focus on the essentials. Don't spend too much time trying to understand or remember every single word in a book. Remember that words are used to communicate ideas and concepts, so focus on those instead. Make notes and highlight those sections that catch your attention, and come back to them again later. Remember that if you spend too much time on one book, you won't have time to read others. Having said that, there are some books, you shouldn't rush through. Books on personal development belong to this category.
- Spend time reflecting on what you've read, and look for opportunities to use the knowledge you've gained. The purpose of reading books here is to help change your thinking, so it's also important to find time to reflect.
- Attend courses, not just for the certificate but to be introduced to new topics —courses and conferences help to kickstart your learning—then it's up to you to explore the topic further.

Time for relationships

No one lives in a vacuum—we all share our lives with the people around us. Our spouses, children, parents, siblings, extended families and friends all play a part in our development, and help us maintain our sanity, just as we do theirs; hence we must not neglect these relationships.

We need to reserves time to spend with our loved ones and to strengthen the bonds. We should also make time to establish new relationships.

Interacting with people is every bit as important as reading books because other people can be an excellent source of information. Some things cannot be learned from books—an hour spent with someone helpful can be worth the information in fifty books. So, make it a point to meet new people regularly. Seek out those relationships not only for what you can get from them, but remember to give something back too. The more we give, the more we get. Our lives are often enriched as much by giving as by receiving.

Time for reflection

We all need time for reflection and self-evaluation. Half of humanity's problems are due to a lack of self-appraisal. As Bob Buford puts it in his book *Half Time*, "man's main problem is that he does not know how to sit quietly in his room." For some of us, this situation is due to the busy lives we lead, but others are scared of reflecting in case they discover truths about themselves they'd rather not know. And yet a period of contemplation can save us a lot of hassle. When we pause and reflect, we give ourselves the chance of spotting our mistakes early, and we correct them before they develop into much bigger problems. When we go through life without reflecting, we end up repeating the same mistakes over and over again. Here are some questions you might want to consider during a period of reflection:

- Am I heading in the right direction?
- Am I on target? Have I been achieving my goals?
- What impact am I having on other people such as clients, target audiences etc. ?
- Is my message getting out loud and clear?
- Have I been neglecting my connections and relationships? Have I been mean to people?
- Have I been neglecting y spiritual life?

It's essential to think about these questions frequently, especially because living a driven life can sometimes lead us to develop tunnel vision. I'd recommend doing this once a week, ideally in a quiet place. Remember to switch off your phone so that you don't end up being distracted.

From time to time, you may want to carry out a much deeper reflection. Book a two or three-day lone holiday, but make sure that the location isn't too busy. Spend time relaxing and reflecting. If you have a life plan or manifesto, then this is the time to review it and add new information. You can also conduct an appraisal using the Self-Appraisal Test in Chapter 2.

Time for recreation

You need time for relaxation. If you're always tensed up trying to find solutions to problems, you'll lose your effectiveness after a while. Regular short breaks can help to renew your strength and "reboot" your mind. Breaks aren't just helpful, they're essential, and you should build them into your work, especially if it involves a lot of thinking. A 5-minute break can bring new ideas, so walk away from your desk from time to time even if it's just to make yourself a drink. When you return to your work, you'll be surprised at how much more effective you are.

You should also go on a long break after several hours of work. I take two kinds of break—I call them *the thinking break* and *the relaxing break*. In a thinking break, I take a specific problem or topic with me. I don't worry about it but ponder it in a different setting. I recommend that you do this too. Try thinking about a problem while taking a shower or out on a walk, for instance. This is not only an efficient use of time (you do two activities in the same time), but it also means that your mind will be active while you're on your break. Think freely about a topic or problem of your choice, and just let your imagination roam.

Such times can be incredibly rewarding, not only leading to new ideas and solutions but also leaving your mind refreshed. I often find that I work more effectively after taking a thinking break.

A relaxation break helps to renew your energies, both mental and physical. You can play a game, watch a movie or do whatever you find relaxing. These kinds of breaks are essential for productivity too. When used wisely, they enable us to return to work with renewed strength, enthusiasm and often with new ideas.

Even while we're relaxing or doing something pleasurable, the mind keeps working in the background, just as an inactive computer does. So your mind might actually be working on a problem while you're watching TV, without you knowing it. You could end up with a solution to a problem you hadn't been thinking about consciously. This accounts for many of our *Eureka* moments, and we can make the most of those moments by always keeping a recording device handy. I always carry my smartphone with me wherever I go to capture new ideas with the voice recording app, as well as to receive phone calls. Why don't you try doing this too? Don't wait till later to write down your idea as you may have forgotten it by then.

Time for fitness

Making the most of your time also means keeping your body in shape. Exercise regularly and eat healthily so your body can serve you well, and for longer, and support the fulfilment of your purpose. Make time for exercise, and make it even more productive by building other activities into it. If you go for a jog or a power walk, take your smartphone or iPod with you and listen to an audiobook while you jog. You can also use that time to think about your projects and record new ideas on your recording device. This way, you may go for a walk and come back with enough material for a chapter of your book!

Make your day go further

There are only 24 hours in a day, but you don't have 24 hours at your disposal—some of that time must be spent doing such things as sleeping, working and using the bathroom etc. Most people sleep for 7 to 8 hours, so that leaves 16 or 17 hours. The commute to work can last an hour or more each way, so that's another two hours gone, bringing the total to 9 or 10 hours with 14 or15 hours left. Take out 8 hours of work, and you have only 6 to 7 hours left. If you cook daily that could take an hour and a half, and because you do these things back-to-back, you're often exhausted by the time you're done. Then, when you sit down to relax, you find yourself snoozing in no time. You go to bed, and that's the whole 24 hours gone. As you can see, a day can pass by without an opportunity to invest in your future. This calls for wise time management. Here are a few tips to help you achieve your goal.

Plan your day beforehand

We cannot emphasise enough how important this is. If you start the day without prior planning, you'll end up filling it with low-value activities that add little to your development; so plan your day in advance. You don't have to plan for every single minute of the day, but you do need to know what your main activity or task will be.

Next, list all the different activities and tasks that need completing. If you're in the middle of a project, then let that be your central task for the day, and plan everything else around it. Allocate time for each activity on your list in such a way that you do the ones requiring high levels of concentration when you're fresh. I find that my mind is sharpest first thing in the morning, or when I've just had a nap, so this is when I carry out tasks that need the maximum focus. I leave the activities requiring less concentration for the afternoon.

Planning your day also means planning your meals. Eat when you're feeling both hungry and tired. If you're hungry at a time when you also feel mentally fresh and want to keep working, then grab a light snack and carry on working. A hot meal may make you lose your freshness, as the mind often dulls after hot meals, especially in the afternoons. This is why many people prefer to have a light lunch. So, grab a snack and keep working. When you really are tired, and ready for a long break, then have a meal. Make eating secondary to your central task.

Try combining activities whenever you can. You could read a book or work on your laptop on the train, or you could listen to an audiobook while you're driving. I know someone who hired a driver as soon as he could afford one. This allowed him to use his travel time even more efficiently. You may not be able to afford a driver yet, but you can still find ways to maximise the time spent travelling in a way that is both safe and within the law.

Finally, structure each day so you have something to do at all times even if it's something relaxing. If you get stuck doing one thing, move on to the next item on your schedule. Don't leave any empty time or it will be filled with a less meaningful activity.

Cut out inefficiencies

Similar activities can be grouped together to save time. If you have to do a few errands in a week, you could lump them together and complete them in one day; ideally, during a break.

Do away with any non-essential activities, and learn to organise your day in the most time-efficient way. This may mean breaking old habits. I used to go for long cycle rides in the mornings, but it often left me feeling exhausted and affected my productivity for the rest of the day. When I realised this, I changed my cycling times.

Maximise your time by engaging in activities when your body and mind are most ready for them. If you notice that your mind is sharper in the mornings, then schedule mental activities for the mornings and do the things that require less concentration later in the day. Be in tune with your body, and maximise its potential.

Get smart with your cooking and shopping

Buy in bulk and cook enough food to last a couple of days. You could precook the meat and then make fresh vegetables when you need them. That could save you a lot of time.

Time your shopping to avoid the busiest hours, this way you can move through the aisles much more quickly. It's often easier to shop late in the evening or early in the morning. Try it! Memorise the shop layout to minimise the time spent looking for things. Finally, you could try online shopping.

Sleep smart

Sleep helps to replenish your energies. It keeps you healthy and helps prepare you for whatever tasks you have next. Don't just sleep because it's night-time. Listen to your body, and attend to its needs. When you're tired, sleep. If not, then get up and work or spend that time reading and studying. Start investing in your future. If you're feeling refreshed after sleeping for 4 hours, don't insist on going back to sleep because it's still dark—get up and work and then go back to bed when you're tired.

Grab a 30-minute nap during the day if you're feeling tired, it'll give you a boost, and you'll be able to work more effectively afterwards. Note that the suggestions in this section presume the absence of any specific medical advice relating to sleep. Make sure you listen to your doctor's advice if you have a medical condition that requires long periods of rest.

Set goals

As we said earlier, having a purpose and limited time within which to achieve it creates a sense of urgency. And you can create that sense of urgency yourself by setting goals for each day. If you set yourself the goal of completing a set of tasks by the end of the day, you'll develop a clear focus and will be able to cut out distractions quite easily. You'll also end up working faster.

Having goals helps prevent procrastination. Most people tend to procrastinate when they have no set time within which to realise their aspirations. This allows us to drift endlessly. So when you set goals, remember to also set a clear timeframe within which to achieve them.

Live mindfully

To live mindfully is to be intentional about life, and to be intentional is to plan and execute rather than just go with the flow. It also means doing things when it's most expedient and not when everyone says you should. You have to learn to say no to people if you want to take control of your life. This can be a hard thing to do, but who said achieving success was easy? It's okay to be spontaneous from time to time and join in when something interesting is happening, but we cannot afford to make this a habit.

Being intentional also means just ignoring your favourite TV show when it's on if you've earmarked that time for something else. You can always record the show and watch it later.

Living mindfully requires you to manage your relationships. Relationships are important, but they're also time-consuming. As soon as you've made a friend, you've also effectively granted them some of your time. That's not a bad thing, but try to be intentional in your contacts with them. Manage your relationships within certain time limits. Make the time you spend with people quality time.

You must absolutely refuse to engage in activities that don't add value. This shouldn't lead to you becoming a recluse; neither should you stop having fun. The point we're making is that everything you do, including recreation, should have a purpose. Recreation is essential, as we've pointed out already. It helps us to relax and regenerate our mental energy. Having fun with other people helps to build relationships, so don't neglect to engage in leisure activities but be intentional about them and plan them. Feel free to say no to suggestions to have fun if you've already earmarked that time for something else. Having fun is important but nowhere near as important as fulfilling your assignment.

Manage time wasters

Every TV set comes with an OFF button, so remember to use it. You weren't born with a disease that makes it imperative to watch TV. If you need to watch TV, watch specialist channels. This way you'll only watch the things you really want to see. If you fancy a documentary, watch an appropriate channel; if you need business news, then watch channels dedicated to business. Switch on the news channel for a brief period to bring you up-to-date with current events. Don't watch 24-hour news channels all day or else you'll end up watching the same thing over and over again, and most of it will be bad news.

Choose catch-up TV rather than live shows. You can also record programmes and watch them later—this way; you'll be able to fast forward the bits you don't want. Many live shows are packed with commercials, so a 30-minute show often ends up lasting an hour. Basketball matches, for instance, last 48 minutes, and yet they can go on for up to two-and-a-half hours because of the breaks and commercials. Look for highlights instead, and watch those if you must. Better still, learn to be content with just the scores.

Key facts:

- Life is time; time is life
- You have a limited time to live on earth
- You cannot have extra time, but you can manage the time you have wisely
- Purpose determines our use of time
- Having clear goals cuts out distractions
- Deadlines help to create a sense of urgency, which cuts out time-wasting
- Planning your day before it arrives also helps to minimise time-wasting
- Live mindfully, and you'll get a lot more done in the same amount of time

Time-management tips

- Set priorities for each day and identify the central task for the day
- Plan your day around your central or main task and make everything else secondary to it
- Work when your body and mind are most ready for that particular type of work
- Listen to your body, and go to bed when you're tired
- Don't sleep just because it's night; sleep because you need to rest
- Have hot meals when you're tired and unable to do mental work.

Chapter 15

Benefitting from adversity

You meant evil against me, but God meant it for good.

Joseph (Gen 50:20 NKJV)

The title of this chapter may come as a shock to some of you. Indeed, I might have argued against it myself if someone had suggested it to me a few years ago. Not anymore. I have come to believe that our challenges, problems and mishaps can propel us to greatness if we know how to benefit from them.

We all see misfortune as something to be avoided at all cost, and to a large extent, it's true. The horrible things that happen to us shouldn't occur; they are in a sense an anomaly. But life has been designed in such a way that nothing should ever go to waste. Therefore, even our worst experiences can become a valuable resource if we can learn to harness the hidden energy within them.

Bad experiences can sweep us away as sea waves do a surfer. Those waves are a death trap to an amateur surfer, but a skilled surfer can ride them all the way to shore. Likewise, if we have the right skills, knowledge and attitudes, then our challenges can propel us on to new heights.

In the story of Joseph, which we referred to in Chapter 4, we see how adversity catapulted him to greatness. When Joseph experienced one problem after another, he kept his head, and above all his heart. First, his brothers wanted to kill him, but they couldn't all agree, so they decided to sell him instead. The Ishmaelite merchants who bought Joseph sold him on to a man named Potiphar, captain of Pharaoh's guard.

For a while, things seemed to go well for Joseph. He won Potiphar's trust and was made his chief butler. But Joseph's stretch of good fortune wouldn't last very long. He'd soon be accused of rape by Potiphar's wife and thrown in jail.

Joseph had every right to throw his toys out of the pram at this point, but he chose instead to maintain a positive attitude. Soon, his leadership skills would begin to manifest, and he'd be made head of the prisoners.

One day, he notices how two of his fellow inmates appear to be troubled. They have each had a dream they cannot interpret. Joseph interprets the dreams, and in due course, these dreams are fulfilled. One of the inmates is released from prison and returns to his duties as the king's cupbearer, just as Joseph had predicted. Upon leaving prison, the man forgets all about Joseph until a dream interpreter is needed two years later. This time, it's Pharaoh who needs his dreams explained. The king's cupbearer recommends Joseph's services to the king, Joseph interprets the king's dreams and is rewarded with a position of honour and power.

This story reveals how the attitude you embrace in adversity will determine the impact it will have on you. Our experiences can make or break us—it all depends on how we approach them. We can adopt a very passive stance, or we can choose to be proactive. We can choose to bemoan our plight, or we can think of ways to benefit from the situation. Unless we maintain a positive attitude, we won't spot the numerous opportunities that adversity brings.

The truth is that every problem comes fully packaged with opportunities. In actual fact, opportunities often come disguised as problems; hence many of us never spot them. Think about how every product or service you see around is a solution to a problem. Mobile phones solve a communication problem, trains solve a transportation problem, and hospitals address health problems. Without the problems, we wouldn't have those products and services.

Amsterdam is a beautiful city crisscrossed by a system of canals. But those canals are a solution to a problem the Dutch have had to grapple with for centuries. Along with a complex system of locks, dykes, and dams, canals help to keep the water levels in check. By addressing the problem of floods, the Dutch have created something to be admired.

Albert Einstein is thought to have said: "Within adversity lies opportunity". To this, I would add that only those who refuse to be beaten by their problems and who concentrate their minds on finding a solution, can benefit from those opportunities.

It was adversity that unearthed Joseph's hidden talents. In his father's house, he'd have ended up as a herdsman just like his brothers—not that there's anything wrong with that. In Egypt, he was exposed to a superior civilisation, and that offered new opportunities.

Because Josef showed himself to be a good steward and leader, both in Potiphar's house and in prison, even greater opportunities opened up for him. Eventually elevated to the equivalent of Prime Minister of Egypt, he would go on to display extraordinary skill in governance. None of those openings would have been available to him in Beersheba where he'd grown up. The truth is that some opportunities arise only in adversity. Some of your skills and talents will only find expression amidst your misfortune.

During the first Gulf War, the Allied forces encountered what they at first thought was bad luck. Out there in the desert with very little cover, and at a time when they'd expected continuous sunshine, there was a downpour of rain that made it impossible to advance for several days. The Allied forces were about to launch an assault on Saddam Hussein's army, and the rain appeared to be a setback, or so they thought. The skies did clear up eventually, giving way to beautiful sunshine, and it was at this point that everyone realised what had happened.

The rainwater had exposed the landmines Saddam's forces had buried in the ground in front of them. What had looked like a problem actually turned out to be their salvation.

This story has since been discounted on one website, but whether it's true or not, there's a lesson to be learnt from it—you don't know what advantages your challenges may bring.

Every destructive force carries energy that can be harnessed for good. The wind, for example, can destroy people's homes, and can also be used to power windmills. Fire is another example. It causes damage to wildlife and property but can be used for cooking and for extracting metal from ore. So don't go through life complaining about your challenges and problems—for all you know there could be hidden treasure within them!

Harnessing the power of adversity

Look outwards

Although there are opportunities aplenty in life, we need to look outward to spot them. But that can be a hard thing to do if you're going through challenges. Our calamities often evoke passivity and self-pity. We lie there helplessly hoping someone would take notice of our suffering and lend a helping hand. We often feel like the world needs to stop for a moment and at least acknowledge our pain. The last thing we want to do is to adopt a positive attitude. And yet, the quickest way out of adversity is to be proactive and seek solutions, and it is by maintaining a positive attitude that we'll spot our opportunities.

To achieve this goal, we must turn our attention away from our problems, and focus on helping someone else with *their* challenges. This may seem counter-intuitive to some, but it forces the mind to enter into problem-solving mode. Being self-focused makes us short-sighted, and the mind operates badly when we're overwhelmed with our own challenges. But fear and worry depart from our hearts when we're helping someone else, and this also frees the shackles on the imagination, making it easier to generate ideas. And in helping someone else, we may, in fact, find solutions to our own problems. So don't let your problems make you too self-focused. Look outwards, and you could solve these problems sooner than you think.

Don't accept your problems

Remember that adversity breeds opportunities, so you shouldn't ever simply accept your problems. Some people have learnt not to complain when they're facing a challenge, and they'll often adapt themselves to the situation. If, for instance, their salary takes a hit, they reduce their spending and carry on in the same job. If they lose their job and can't find another one that pays a similar salary, they go for a lower-paid job instead. In other words, they lower their expectations to cope with the situation. Obviously, this is a better approach than to sit there complaining about your plight while doing nothing about it. But you can find a better way, and really make the most of the situation.

When you encounter a new challenge ask: what's this situation trying to teach me? If you've just lost your job, then ask whether you'd have been fired if you had different qualifications. Find out if a different set of skills and qualifications would give you an edge over other job seekers, and whether your current location is best suited to finding the kind of work you're after. Ask yourself whether you need a job, or if you should be trying your hand at setting up your own business instead. Be prepared to dig deep and think outside the box at the same time, because if anything, that's what adversity is supposed to do; it is supposed to help you think differently about life and about your situation.

Mine those diamonds

If someone asked you to dig a hole with only a spade, and you discovered that the ground was full of rocks, you wouldn't be very thrilled about it. However, if you found out there were diamonds hidden under the rocks, your attitude would change. You'd consider hiring a digger or a worker to help you do a thorough job. You'd begin to think outside the box.

You may have gone through life moaning about your predicament, but now you know that adversity contains resources, you should change your attitude. You can start looking for ways to make the most of your situation.

Richer than you think

Life on earth has been designed in such a way as to provide each one of us with opportunities even if all we have is problems. We all have something that can be turned to our advantage, so we don't need to envy anyone else.

Our failures can open doors to far greater riches than our successes ever will. People often celebrate their accomplishments and get little else from them. Sportsmen and women get complacent after scoring major victories and end up losing the momentum they'd previously gathered. Students stop studying after they've passed their exams, and in some cases, they quickly forget everything they'd learned. In other words, our successes often bring very limited benefits.

Our failures, on the other hand, come with a bountiful supply of opportunities. If we fail an exam and resit it, we end up learning more than the guy who passed it the first time around. Our flops teach us to be humble and more understanding of other people's mistakes. Humility is an invaluable asset to have if we want to succeed in life.

Even some of the things that can kill you can bring benefits. Everyone knows that snake poison kills, but did you know that it can also save lives? The very chemical that causes uncontrolled bleeding after a snake bite can also be used as a blood thinner to treat blood clotting diseases.

Problems can be like the hardest flint that contains precious gems— crack it open, and the resources are bountiful! So don't be discouraged by your failures; neither let your problems overwhelm you. Don't contemplate retreat because of the obstacles you're currently facing. Take time out to reflect. Ask questions, and try to understand your situation. Speak to someone who's been through similar challenges and has experienced a positive outcome. Learn what you can from them and then have another go at solving your problems.

Don't dwell on past mistakes

We're sometimes the architects of our own misfortunes. Some of us have taken decisions that we now regret. Some of those decisions have led to suffering, not only for ourselves but for other people too. How do we get around that? Often, our approach is to blame ourselves and ruminate as if to atone for our mistakes with the accompanying feeling of regret. But regret does not make up for past mistakes, neither does guilt. These feelings merely inform us that something isn't quite right and that where possible; we should make an effort to restore normality. Once that message has been understood, we ought to shed negative feelings and focus our efforts on bringing about the change that they demand.

While we're dwelling on our mistakes, our minds are not free to critically examine why we made these mistakes in the first place, so we'll be in danger of repeating them. This is why some people can never break free from recidivist behaviour. They do regret their actions, but that's about it. They dwell on their regrets for a while until their circumstances change, and a more compelling argument forces them to commit that very crime once again. Feelings of guilt and regret alone cannot change anybody. Dwelling on them won't make you a better person. You may appear endearing to others for being remorseful, but unless you understand why you made your mistakes, you're likely to repeat them. This is why we need to strip away the feelings of guilt and regret we have about our mistakes and use these mistakes as case studies instead. We need to study them intensely until we understand why we keep making them, and only then will we develop a new approach and avoid repeating our typical mistakes.

Avoid common traps

I once met a man after he'd been medically discharged from the army. He'd suffered an injury in training and was deemed unfit to continue. Since his ambition had been to have a career in the army, life for him had effectively come to a standstill. He was in self-destruct mode when I met him—the injury and subsequent rejection by the army had transformed into a mental handicap preventing him from accessing his resources, of which he had plenty. He was still, by and large, an able-bodied man with a sharp intellect; yet he felt that he had nothing to offer the world. This is someone who let his bad experiences hold him back.

The world is not a perfect place. Things happen that shouldn't happen. None of us has control over those things, but we can control how things affect us. We can limit the impact of the calamities that we experience by choosing how we react when they happen. We can spend the rest of our lives bemoaning our bad luck, or we can pick ourselves up and make the most of the situation. This is how the rest of creation operates. You can cut down a tree, but unless you also dig up the roots, it will attempt to grow back up. It won't give up on life just because it has lost years of hard work. As long as it has roots, it will attempt to grow again. Animals make the most of their lives while nursing the severe injuries inflicted by humans or other animals. They know the secret of never giving up.

If you're lucky enough to have a problem-free life, then enjoy it, but the chances are, you will face some problems at various times. We all have our fair share of problems and calamities, and it's up to us to decide whether to be bitter or better. It's tempting to sit there and lament the unfairness of life, but many have been down this path before and have only reaped misery. Self-pity won't get you anywhere. It will only make you neglect your resources—if life knocks you back, quickly dust yourself down and move on. Don't allow the situation to register in your mind as a disadvantage or handicap; otherwise, you'll have to fight a long battle to rid yourself of hang-ups. Remember that the wrong mindset is the worst disability you could possibly have.

Key facts:

- Every problem comes with opportunities
- Every destructive force carries energy that can be harnessed for good
- Your mindset determines the effect your adversities will have on you
- Don't let adversities register in your mind as handicaps, but when they happen, quickly dust yourself down and move on
- Don't ruminate over past mistakes, but use them as case studies to learn what you can from them
- Don't accept having problems
- Let problems spur you on to think outside the box

Some points to consider:

- How have you been responding to your challenges?
- Do you try to learn from your challenges or do you sit back and bemoan your bad luck?
- What challenges are you facing right now?
- What lessons should you be learning from them?

Chapter 16

Make the most of your opportunities!

We're very fortunate to be living in the 21st Century. We have resources and opportunities that generations before us didn't have. Before the advent of the internet and social media, you had to jump through many hoops to get noticed. But today, you can have your own website, social media page, YouTube channel or blog. You can also conduct live broadcasts and post videos on the internet. There has never been a better time to showcase your talent, and the truth is that unless you do, no one will take any notice of you. Why not let people know about your amazing gift, and show yourself to the world?

Years ago people couldn't always profit from their inventions because there were no suitable platforms available for showcasing their achievements. In some cases, their accomplishments went completely unnoticed. But with all the different platforms now that needn't happen to you.

Get out there!

Do you like cooking? Is cooking one of your strengths? Why not start a culinary show on YouTube? You could begin by posting videos of yourself preparing meals and demonstrating different cooking techniques. You could invite viewers to leave questions and suggestions for your next video in the comments section. This encourages them to participate in what you're doing, which will generate more interest.

Remember to ask them to *like* your videos and subscribe to your channel. If this is something you're genuinely interested in, then get started!

Check out YouTube, and you'll find videos on how to start a channel. You'll also find ideas about how to attract viewers and make your channel popular. Someone has gone out of their way to make it really easy for you to showcase your talent, and for free! So, what's your excuse going to be for not trying? The worst thing that can happen is that someone may not like your videos, but why care about that? With over 7 billion people in the world today, someone somewhere is going to love it.

Remember to make your videos stand out by adding in little extras. Some time ago, I came across some YouTube videos giving lessons in the Akan language. The presenter began each lesson with a quick word about how her week had gone. Sometimes, she'd do a little dance as she spoke and it made her videos really interesting to watch. If you decide to add in such little touches, make sure you stay true to yourself—don't try to copy anyone else. You can also include a personal element such as bringing a member of your family to the show. Viewers really enjoy this sort of thing!

Take your smartphone when you go on holiday, and film yourself roaming through the market shopping for ingredients to cook with. Many TV chefs do this, and viewers love it. Asking viewers to suggest topics will generate even more interest in your videos. Make this a regular activity, so you don't lose your following. As you build a following, you can start writing a culinary blog, and direct your viewers to your blog.

And if you're not sure about writing the blogs yourself, why not hire someone to do it for you? There are ghostwriters out there who will write your blog for a small fee. Try www.fiver.com or www.upwork.com, and you'll find many freelance writers ready to help you fulfil your dream. All you need to do is give them an outline of what you want to write about and a few salient details. You can even write a cookery book this way. There's really no excuse for not showing the world what you can do.

Interior design

Some people are naturally gifted in design. Their homes look like showhouses, and their gardens look great too. What they don't know is that there are people wishing their homes were that pretty, and who are willing to pay someone to design and decorate for them. Either they just haven't got round to organising it yet, or they're hesitant to hire a professional, fearing that it would cost a fortune. This situation opens up a business opportunity. If you're gifted in this type of work, you could step in and offer your services.

You could begin with friends and do the work for free on condition that they let you showcase your work. Redecorate their homes, take photos, and have them published in a magazine or on specialist websites. Alternatively, you could set up a website yourself.

If photography isn't one of your strengths, then hire a professional. And instead of using your local photographer, who may not specialise in interiors and might be expensive, why not look up freelance photographers on the internet? Get one who specialises in interior design if that's what you want to showcase. Upload the pictures onto your website or social media page. If you get a lot of positive comments, take things a step further.

You can also upload photos of homes you've decorated on YouTube and similar platforms. If you get a good response, go from there and start charging for your services.

Read about interior design and subscribe to interior-design magazines. Visit showrooms, trade fairs, and have a look at interior design websites. Start collating ideas, and draw inspiration from what you see to help you create new designs. If you'd like to pursue this as a career, then consider going on a course.

Mentoring

Raising children is one of the hardest tasks these days, and so many parents struggle with it. If you've managed to raise well-behaved children, then there's an opportunity for you. You could set up a parent advisory service. It sounds rather lofty, but it isn't at all. In the days when most people lived in small, close-knit communities, older, more experienced women often mentored the younger ones in bringing up their children. Unfortunately, we've lost this now as most of us live in cities, and are isolated from other members of our communities. As a consequence, many young people become parents without knowing how to raise a child, and some of them labour under a lot of guilt because they feel they're not doing a good job.

If your children have turned out well, you could become a mentor for young parents and parents-to-be. Start writing blogs about parenting, highlighting the challenges you faced as a parent and how you overcame them. You could also post videos on the internet where you talk about these issues. As you build a following and your audience begins to show interest in accessing your services, you could start offering an advisory service via video chat. You could also set up an internet support group, and possibly follow it up with a face-to-face group.

The challenges of parenting are having a knock-on effect on societies across the globe, but attempts by the state to tackle them don't work, which is hardly surprising. Problems of this nature are best addressed by ordinary citizens like you and I—so why not step into that gap and help bring about a solution? Many would be eternally grateful if you did. In some countries, the government provides funding to assist those tackling such problems. Find out if there are such opportunities where you live and if you'd qualify for funding.

Homeschooling

Homeschooling offers opportunities too, although to be honest, I can't quite understand how one can raise their children and be in charge of their education as well. Raising them seems to me a hard enough task. Nevertheless, many parents have not only managed this successfully, but their children have scored top grades in their exams and gained admission into top universities. So why aren't they talking about it? If a school did that, it would make sure its achievements were well publicised.

Here's my suggestion: if you've homeschooled your children successfully, consider helping someone else do the same. Many parents would like to homeschool their children but don't know how to go about it. Some of them are unhappy with the education system, while others have children who've had bad experiences at school and have stopped attending as a result. So, why not step in and come to the rescue? You could start writing blogs about homeschooling and share your story. You could explain how to start a homeschool, and share tips on how to overcome daily challenges. You could organise seminars and networking events to bring other homeschoolers together. And once you've built up momentum, you could even start a consultancy and charge for your services.

Nurseries

Additionally, a lot of parents find the traditional preschools and kindergartens inadequate for their children's needs. They want something customised to their needs and preferences and are willing to pay for it. This could be an opportunity for you. If you're good with children and you're interested in childcare, why not take steps in that direction? Find out what formal qualifications you need, and train to be a preschool teacher or a childminder. Apply for a job in a nursery and watch how things are done. Find out how to set up a nursery, and set one up yourself. Give people a reason for choosing yours by making it unique.

These are only a few of the opportunities available. There are literally hundreds, but you have to be ready to search for them. Note that we haven't suggested you get a job to showcase your talents. Unfortunately, it isn't very often that we get to use our God-given talents in our jobs; there are often too many restrictions. But if you're able to put your talents to good use in your job, then by all means, remain there—think of ways of reaching more people with what you do at the same time. If this is not in your employer's best interest, you may need to extend your activities beyond the workplace. Whatever you decide, remember to do some research first—don't just jump in at the deep end!

Chapter 17

How to plan, start and complete a project

In this chapter, we'll continue the discussion on how to make your dream come true. But first I'd like to commend everyone who has already decided to make their dreams a reality. Most people never get to this stage. Dreaming can be very gratifying, and some people do it every day, but without ever taking that crucial step towards fulfilment. So well done for getting to this stage!

For any dream to become a reality, you need a plan. To produce a workable plan though, you'll have to leave behind the imaginary world of fantasies and engage your imagination in the here and now instead. If, for instance, you aspire to owning a business, you should start thinking about how to go about it, and what you would need to start it. You should consider practicalities such as capital, location, day to day operations, marketing, sales and cash flow. You need to pose questions about each of these areas and make sure you find the answers you need. You cannot go from a fabulous idea to successful implementation without going through this stage. But before you get to this stage, you need to be clear about your aims.

Define your aims and objectives

Any project you decide to undertake will doubtless involve problem-solving. This is as true of not-for-profit ventures as it is of businesses. Your product or service will solve a problem, and this will be your aim.

For a community project, the aim might be getting youngsters off the streets or addressing antisocial behaviour. Unless you have a clear aim, you might lose your focus.

The next thing to remember is to stick with your aim and let it guide your every action. You need to regularly reflect on your actions, and ensure they align with the aim of the project. If you don't, there'll be a danger that the project will become an end in itself. Many social initiatives suffer this fate. They start out as movements meant to address a specific social problem but soon morph into ultra-bureaucratic organisations with huge operational costs. Often, their internal activities end up overshadowing their aims and objectives.

Study the problem

If your goal is to tackle antisocial behaviour in your area, then you'll need to find out how it started, what has kept it going, and who's involved. You'll also need to study the habits of those involved and find out whether there's a ringleader. The effect of boredom, inadequate parental supervision, the influence of organised crime groups, and the role of drugs and alcohol would all need to be explored.

For a project like this, you'd need to learn about the psyche of youths in general and those who get involved in antisocial behaviour in particular. You'd need to look out for any specific traits that make the young people in your area prone to this behaviour, and this would require a lot of reading and research.

You'd also need to spend time observing the behaviour as it happens, and speak to people in the area. You'd need to be careful how you went about it though, so as not to give the impression that you were snooping.

Finally, you should consider the problem carefully, and allow your imagination free rein. You'd then need to ask the three most important questions in life: what, why and how.

What?

- What problem are you trying to solve? It's essential to define the problem very clearly as the solution may not be applicable otherwise. Ask yourself whether you're more concerned about the plight of the youths in your area or more interested in the welfare of the victims. Ideally, you want to address both, but you might not have the means to do so, so you'd need to be clear about which one was a priority.

- What might a good solution be? Do some brainstorming. Be bold and let your imagination run wild. Ask yourself how you'd tackle this problem if money, time and resources weren't an issue. This will remove the limitations from your imagination, and you'll be able to generate ideas more easily. You can also ask friends and family for their ideas of how they'd address the problem.
- Are there better options than the ones you're thinking about? Always throw the net as wide as possible, and think beyond the obvious.

Why?

The only legitimate reason for starting any venture is to address a problem. Although this should be obvious to all of us, this is often not the case. The reason is that human motivation derives from multiple sources. Sometimes, people start projects not because the projects themselves are needed, but because some people need to prove something to themselves. Boredom and a lack of purpose can also drive our actions, but this kind of motivation means we're liable to abandon our projects if something more exciting comes along.

To avoid this scenario, it's worth taking the time to identify your *why* before plunging into any endeavour. It will save you from making a false start. Consider the following questions:

- Why are you undertaking this project?
- Do you sense in it a calling or is it an assignment you can really commit yourself to? Or alternatively, are you doing it just to satisfy your ego?
- Are you starting this endeavour because you're bored?
- Is this project an attempt to prove to yourself that you're not a failure?

- Is it an attempt to carve out a purpose for your life? Remember that you must first have a purpose and then use your project to achieve it; not the other way around.
- Is there a market for the product or solution you're trying to develop?
- What could be the consequences of pursuing or not pursuing your idea?

How?

How questions are technical ones. They're about planning. Asking these questions will enable you to create the project, product or service in your mind before making it a reality. *How* questions help to turn an idea into a clear plan. Below are a few that are worth considering:

- How might your idea solve the problem? Starting a project can be an exciting thing to do, but to avoid failure you need to examine your idea critically to see if it would work. Let your excitement cool off and then do some imaginative thinking. Imagine the solution being implemented. Note how people respond to it and look out for the obstacles that emerge.
- How might the idea be implemented? Visualise yourself rolling out the project from beginning to end. Be meticulous and note down every step it would involve.
- What resources do you need and where might you find them? Think about time, money and people. Also, remember that you are your own greatest resource. Ask yourself whether you can commit yourself fully to your venture—and give it your all.
- Who do you need to involve? Think about the people you're going to need in the planning stage as well as in the implementation stage. Think about the specific skills they need to bring to the table to supplement yours. Consider what their motives might be for joining the project, and what you need to do to get them involved.
- Are there any existing solutions you can adopt? Would they work as they are or do they need tweaking?

If you're trying to set up a business or service, you'll also need to answer the following questions:

- Who are you trying to reach with your product or service? What does your target client look like?
- What might a client look for in your product or service?
- Who is your competition? How does your product compare with theirs?

Get inside knowledge

It's always helpful to have friends and family by your side when you're starting a project. Their words of encouragement can see you through the hard times. But you also need the support of someone who has inside knowledge and can tell you how the buses run, as it were, what opportunities to look out for, and which traps to avoid. Their advice can save you a lot of hassle.

If you're trying to start a business, you need to enlist the help of an entrepreneur. Ideally, it should be someone who's in the type of business that you want to start. You might want to hire a business coach if you can afford one, but often, you can get a lot of tips for free if you befriend business people. You can find them at business forums, and at your local chamber of commerce. Google it!

Additionally, your local chamber of commerce can directly provide you with advice and assistance. In some countries, there are also designated institutions for assisting startups. Finally, there's plenty of free advice online if you know what you're looking for and can ask the right questions. Check out some of the question-and-answer sites for businesses.

You could consider taking an apprenticeship if your project requires a skill that you need to acquire. If you take up employment with a company that makes something similar to what you want to produce or design, you'll be able to learn about their approach. I know someone who did just that. If you choose to go down this route, make sure you know what you're looking for; otherwise, it could end up being a waste of time.

Generate enthusiasm for your project

Imagine that you're preparing for a marathon. You've begun your preparation by reading about it, which by the way, is how you ought to approach everything. Let's say that the book you've chosen focuses on the challenges involved, and tells some gruesome stories about people who tried to run the marathon and failed. To your horror, you learn that some even died as a result. Now, in this imaginary situation, would you still feel as enthusiastic about the marathon as you had before reading the book? Probably not! Chances are, you're beginning to think twice about it, and that's because you started your learning with negative information.

It's important to learn about the potential obstacles before you start any project, but *when* you learn about them is equally vital. If your idea is unsafe and utterly unrealistic, then you need a reality check rather than encouragement. Learning about potential challenges early on can usher in a healthy dose of realism and save you a lot of trouble. But on the whole, it isn't a good idea to learn about the obstacles at the outset as this might make you doubt the validity of the project altogether. Many ventures have failed to take off for this very reason. This is why I'm going to suggest a very different approach.

Instead of learning about the obstacles, give your attention to positive information, and generate enthusiasm for your project. This will put your mind in a *can-do* mode, and make it easier to face the obstacles you'll learn about later. If you start with the obstacles, fear and discouragement may fill your heart and stifle your creativity, preventing the flow of ideas.

In the case of a marathon, read inspiring accounts of people who've successfully completed the marathon. Visualise doing that yourself, and focus on that imagery until it becomes real. Only then should you consider the challenges. In other words, the approach I'm recommending is to first work hard to see a clear path to the fulfilment of your dream before you turn your attention to the potential obstacles.

Plan it

Have you ever attended an event, only to find the whole place in disarray and everyone confused about what was going on? The most likely explanation is that the organiser probably hadn't visualised the event before it happened. Let me explain.

Most people planning an event understand the importance of nailing the logistics, and so they're likely to put some thought into securing the right venue, drawing up an event programme, hiring a catering firm and making sure that the venue is ready on the day. These things, which are fairly easy to organise, I'll refer to as the *static factors*. If you're planning a conference for 50, for example, you obviously need a conference room with at least 50 seats. Knowing the number of delegates would also make it easier to work out the amount of food and drinks to purchase.

But there are other aspects of planning that can't be worked out so easily. You couldn't tell, for instance, whether the delegates would arrive on time or whether the event would overrun. This kind of information can only be surmised by imagining what might happen. You should visualise the whole event from start to finish, and break it down into stages. For a conference, these stages would be: pre-event preparations, the arrival and registration of delegates, the main event, the round up at the end, and finally the departure from the event venue.

The next step is to imagine what could go wrong at each stage. If your conference clashes with another big event or a planned protest match, then members of your team, as well as the delegates, may have difficulty getting to the venue. This could delay the preparations as well as the event itself. By thinking about the journey to the venue, you'll be able to take into account any eventualities. A quick phone call to the police department would reveal whether there are any protests planned. You can also find out about roadblocks and disruptions to the public transport network by phoning the appropriate authorities.

The EUFA Champions League may be one of the greatest football spectacles in the world, second in magnitude only to the World Cup. Yet one of its matches was delayed due, most probably, to poor foresight. On 2 October 2018, the Manchester United players arrived late for their match against Valencia at the Theatre of Dreams (the Manchester

United stadium). The team had anticipated, as the club officials had told them, that the drive to the stadium would take 30 minutes. It turned out that the heavy traffic that day meant it took 75 minutes. The club management had failed to visualise the worst-case scenario. The next time, the manager Jose Mourinho decided that he would stay in a hotel next to the stadium the night before, to avoid being late for the match. He'd learned from the previous experience. As for the team preparations were made for an earlier arrival.

The point we're making is that it's always essential to consider the worst-case scenarios when planning an event and make preparations for them. This will save you a lot of hassle later.

Your event information pack should include maps and instructions showing people how to get to the venue. Before you finalise those instructions, test them out yourself. Put yourself in a delegate's shoes and follow the instructions to check that they're clear.

If the event is taking place in an obscure location, it's important that you or a designated member of your team knows the area well. Take a drive around and form a mental image of the area. This will make it easier to direct those who get lost. If feasible, leave clear signs directing delegates to the venue. Create an information pack that includes directions on how to get there for your receptionists or anyone taking phone calls from delegates.

Pre-event preparation for a conference should involve learning all you can about the delegates' needs before they arrive. You could send them all a short questionnaire about specific dietary needs, e.g. gluten-free diet, vegetarian or vegan diets. You could also use this opportunity to inform them about local attractions and a few of the limitations of the event venue, such as the lack of a cloakroom or storage facilities for suitcases for those travelling. It's no good letting people arrive with their suitcases only to find that there's nowhere to put them.

For the event itself, you need to allocate enough time for each agenda item. You need to have a plan in place to prevent the agenda items from overrunning.

To minimise disruptions, you should visualise the behaviour of the delegates from the moment of arrival up to departure, and factor in such details as the use of toilets, and the queuing up for food and drinks during breaks. You also need to have members of your team on hand to help with enquiries.

The movement of delegates in and out of the event venue during an emergency would also be an important consideration. This is likely to be covered by standard health and safety procedures for the venue, but you need to factor in anything else that might make it particularly difficult to evacuate some of the delegates, e.g. disabilities.

Finally, you need to visualise the logistics involved in the event closure, including the transport for delegates.

Build a team

Unless your project is straightforward, you're probably going to need someone's help to complete it, so you need to think about who your helpers will be. For one-off projects such as events, you can hire people to help you. By visualising each step, you'll be able to identify the number of people you need on your team.

You need a second-in-command so that there's someone to take charge when you're not around. For a small project, a friend or a member of your family may suffice. If you belong to a church or a social group, you could look there for a helper too. Your second-in-command should know as much as you do about the project and be equally enthusiastic about it. They need to join the project early; otherwise, they might not attract the same level of trust and respect as you do.

Execute

Getting your project off the ground can be a challenge, especially if you haven't done it before. It's possible that you might get everything ready to start but still lack the impetus to take off. This is often due to a fear of failure, and you can overcome this obstacle by generating enthusiasm at the beginning. Like a wave, it will carry you over any obstacles, and help you overcome the initial inertia.

Remember to maintain your excitement about the project. Don't get so bogged down with the details that you lose your enthusiasm.

A perfectionist approach can be an impediment to starting a

project. Some people won't act unless everything is just right. But one of the rewards in life is in learning from your mistakes and making improvements after each false start. Don't let the pursuit of perfection hold you back! Use what you have to get started—you'll get better as you gain experience. Read *Start Now Get Perfect Later* by Rob Moore. This book thoroughly addresses the problem of procrastination.

Legislate for failure

> *I have not failed 10,000 times—I've successfully found 10,000 ways that will not work.*

Thomas Edison

Imagine you've lost your way while out hiking in the forest. There are trails, but many of them are not marked, so it's very confusing. You have your smartphone with you, but there's no signal, and the map app doesn't seem to be working well. After labouring unsuccessfully for half-an-hour, you spot a footpath that could lead to your destination. But after following it for about 10 minutes, you end up in the wrong place, next to a lake. Frustrated, you retrace your steps and look for another trail, but that seems to take you round and round, and you end up where you began.

What would you do in this situation? Would you give up or look for another trail? I bet that's an easy question to answer. You wouldn't give up just because your previous attempts at finding the right route failed. You'd tell yourself there *was* a way out of the forest—there was a way in after all, and so you'd keep looking. Why not approach your project in the same way?

Many people give up on their dreams after a few failed attempts to realise them, but that's not the approach Thomas Edison took. He treated his failures as part of the process of achieving his aim, and after thousands of failed experiments, he succeeded in inventing the light bulb. His persistence paid off.

Persistence always pays off; if nothing else, it helps us to develop strength of character, and that alone can bring us success. So, don't give up if your project hits a stumbling block or fails. Take time to understand why that happened, and start again. Keep trying until you succeed, and treat each failure as a learning opportunity.

Allow for failure. Make room for the possibility of your first few attempts not succeeding. Create a buffer in your budget and allocate time and other resources for any eventualities—this is called contingency planning. If it works the first time around, that's great! If not, you'll not be disheartened. Having a contingency plan will reduce the likelihood of you abandoning your project after a false start.

Build momentum

Starting a project can be challenging for all the reasons we've mentioned; yet opportunities to stall, once you've got going, are never in short supply. The main challenge is in maintaining your motivation. Lack of resources may also play a role, although if you're determined, then you'll always find them.

The way to keep your motivation is by building up momentum. Momentum is the impetus or force that is generated by motion. A stationary object has no momentum, but as soon as it starts moving, it begins to exert a force, and as it accelerates that force increases. It is hard to stop an object when it's moving at full speed. If you stand in its way, you'll get knocked over. That's the effect of momentum.

The same law applies to processes too. A project that has gathered momentum is difficult to stop. Therefore, if you want to overcome the resistance that we all face when we start a project, you should learn to generate momentum.

How to build it

One of the keys to building momentum is to make the project your principal focus. It should take centre stage in your daily schedule, and you should be thinking about it even when you're not actually working on it. You need to consider it during your meals, when you're having a shower, while out on a walk, and in bed, before you sleep. It should always be your dominant thought.

Your project also needs to be your principal activity. All other engagements should take second place. Cut out any unnecessary meetings, and feel free to say "No" to any non-essential demands on your time.

We all need recreation and relaxation, but you should keep these to a bare minimum while you're trying to generate momentum for your project. Remember that leisure activities at the wrong time can knock you off-course. Anything can be a distraction when you're trying to get a project off the ground. That's why someone like Thomas Edison often hid himself away in his laboratory for weeks while working on his projects. Such people aren't weird—they know the secret of momentum and understand the necessity of being wholly committed to their endeavours to the exclusion of all else. Otherwise, they'll lose either their motivation or their focus.

You may not have the chance to seclude yourself as Thomas Edison and others have done, but you *can* embrace some of the principles that made them successful. So, avoid unnecessary chit chat with those around you, and leave your hobbies for now. Keep all social interactions and phone calls to a minimum, including those with friends and family. Give them your attention at some other time, when you're not trying to generate momentum. Explain how important it is that you focus only on the project, and then get on with it; they'll understand. If you were preparing for an exam, they'd understand and leave you to study.

I hasten to add that this is not a recipe for life, but only for the initial stages of your project. When you've built enough momentum to the point that nothing can distract you, then start factoring in time for other things.

Don't worry about other people's reactions while you're trying to generate momentum. Take no notice of the disapproving looks on their faces. Keep your head down and go on working. Some people feel a little uncomfortable when they see someone else completely obsessed with something. If you take too much notice of their reactions, you might start questioning what you're doing and end up losing momentum.

Work back-to-back

Another key to building momentum is to minimise the number of breaks you take from your work. When we work back-to-back, we cover more ground in a shorter time. If you work for 4 hours with very short breaks, you'll get a lot more done than if you worked for 4 hours over three days. The reason is that when we spread out the work, we often have to recap.

If you were writing a book and took a week's break from it, you'd need to refresh your memory before resuming the writing. That would take time. But you wouldn't need to do this if you were working back-to-back.

For this reason, you should align the various steps in your project to ensure you have something to do at all times. Wake up each morning and tell yourself that there's work to be done—and then get on with it! Don't allow gaps of more than several hours at a time in between; otherwise, they'll be filled with resistance, and you'll lose your enthusiasm and motivation to continue as a result. And unless you're very diligent, you're liable to abandon the project.

Streamline your work in such a way that if you hit a bottleneck, you can move on to another aspect of the project and carry on working. Don't allow yourself to get stuck—if you're trying to design a product and hit an obstacle, leave it and start working on marketing or packaging instead. Come back to the product design later with a fresh mind, and you'll have new ideas.

Don't insist on resolving any bottlenecks there and then; otherwise you might get frustrated if you're unable to find a solution. And your frustration might turn into discouragement.

Many problems work themselves out if you're patient enough with them, so move on to a different aspect of the project if you hit an obstacle, and come back to it later. The problem may prove surprisingly easy to solve a few days later.

Never allow the momentum you've generated to drop. Keep pushing forward.

Complete your project

There's always a temptation to abandon a project before it's complete. This happens all the time, and as we've explained, it's because of the resistance we face. Some of this will come from people, but your own mind will resist you too. After the initial burst of enthusiasm has died down, you may find yourself pondering every possible excuse under the sun to abandon your project.

The way to overcome this problem is to make yourself accountable to someone. Tell a person you trust and respect about your project, and ask them to question you about it. Anytime they ask about your progress; it will be a reminder to keep going. I've used this approach with this book, and the fact that you're reading it now is proof that it works.

It also helps to set time-limited goals. If you break the project down into stages and set a deadline for completing each stage, you'll find it easier to stay on track.

Finally, remember why you're undertaking the project in the first place. Think about the problem you're trying to solve, the lives your project will transform, the profits you'll make, and the fact that it's your assignment. Focus on these positive aspects of it, and not on the challenges.

Don't be deterred by negative attitudes either. Remember that few feats have ever been achieved with unanimous approval. Don't expect your endeavour to draw applause. If you rely too much on approbation, you'll also end up being affected more easily by the criticisms you encounter. Moreover, opinions change with results—those who were once your worst critics will support you when things start working out.

Key facts:

- To start a project you must have clear goals
- Solving a problem needs to be your overarching aim
- Start your project by trying to understand the problem
- Brainstorm for ideas and make sure those ideas are workable
- Identify the resources you need, and build a team

- Don't stall, execute!
- Generate momentum by cutting out distractions and by focusing on your project
- Work back-to-back
- Legislate for failure
- Complete your task

Chapter 18

Getting past obstacles

Anyone who wants to be successful in life needs to know that they'll have to overcome challenges before they can achieve their goals. This is a fact of life. A stationary object encounters little or no resistance, but a moving one does. Machines have to overcome friction to get going, and athletes need to work against gravity to run faster or jump higher. Nothing worth having ever comes easily.

On the other hand, you'll face little opposition if you choose to do nothing meaningful with your life. The young guy sitting on his couch eating crisps and chocolate bars all day isn't going to face much opposition except for his mum nagging him every now and then to get his act together. But let him start doing something useful with his life, and the problems will start to emerge. He'll need to overcome them if he wants to make any headway. Like him, you'll face many challenges when trying to bring meaningful change to his life. These challenges will come from three sources: the environment, other people and your own mind. We'll now address each in turn.

Everyone hates me

To lift an object, you must first overcome gravity, and to move the object, you need to overcome friction. Gravity and friction oppose our actions, yet that isn't their primary role. Gravity attaches objects to the surface of the earth and prevents them from drifting off into space; whereas friction ensures firm contact between objects thus preventing them from sliding against each other. These two forces of nature work together to provide stability and ensure safety. When we try to work against them, they resist us. If you lean against an object to move it, it pushes back as it were. Isaac Newton described this as action and reaction. The harder you hit an object, the more it hurts.

If you try to introduce a change into your environment, you can expect pushbacks from those whom the changes will affect. But like the forces of nature, not everyone who opposes you would be doing it deliberately to stop you. Most people don't like change, and when they sense it coming, they resist it. If you tell your spouse that you're about to embark on a journey of self-discovery or start to fulfil your dreams, he or she will wonder what that might mean for them. You can be certain that your plans will cause anxiety, which might lead to opposition. They wouldn't necessarily be doing it to stop you, but to oppose change. Therefore, expect some opposition to your good intentions, but don't be deterred by it. Instead, learn to make the most of it by pushing to resist the force (but without offending anyone).

The benefits of resistance

Have you ever driven down a country road? Did you notice how different it was from driving on a motorway or highway? Motorways are often arrow-straight. They're designed for speed and long-distance travel, and they make driving easy. You don't have to do much on the motorway apart from keeping your foot on the pedal and staying alert. This also means that it is easier to switch off. If anyone is likely to fall asleep behind the wheel, it's likely to be on the motorway.

Driving in the countryside is a different ball game, however. For starters, the roads have a lot of bends—some of them very sharp—which calls for caution. You must also keep an eye out for other motorists, tractors, and occasionally, horse carriages joining the motorway from side roads. In Australia, you might come across animals in the middle of the road in no hurry to make way for you. There are challenges on every corner, and the only way to stay safe is to keep your eyes open. Indeed, the obstacles on the road help to keep you awake.

It's the same in life: the obstacles we come across each day keep us on our toes. When everything seems to be going well, we become complacent and switch off. When we encounter obstacles though, we're often forced to think harder to come up with a solution, and in many cases, we end up with ideas we might not have thought of otherwise.

Overcoming obstacles helps to build character

Bodybuilders rely on the forces of gravity and friction for a good workout. Gravity gives objects their weight, and friction makes it possible to get a good grip. Without friction, the weights would slip out of the bodybuilder's hands and cause injury; whereas, without gravity, he couldn't build up any muscle. Likewise, the challenges we face help to shape our character. When we work hard to overcome them, we develop the moral fibre needed for life. Traits such as patience, perseverance and resilience are enhanced as we endure challenges. So, don't let obstacles stop you from fulfilling your assignment. Let them bring out the best in you!

Obstacles help to improve our skills

When someone opposes us, we can bulldoze them with the sheer force of our arguments, but we can also allow the situation to teach us the skill of dealing with people. That skill alone can bring us success.

A sculptor, working with stone could strike it with a heavy tool and split it into pieces, but the end result would not be a work of art. On the other hand, if he chose a subtler tool and worked with less force, he could produce a piece that would draw admiration. In both cases, he'll have overcome resistance, but with the latter approach, he'll have perfected his skills. Likewise, the opposition we face can fine-tune our people skills and help us deal with future challenges.

Overcoming resistance brings satisfaction:

Without challenges and obstacles, we sometimes feel like a fraud. Imagine being in a weightlifting competition where gravity works only on your opponents' weights. While they toil to lift theirs, your weights are as light as a feather, and in the end, you win the competition without even breaking into a sweat. You're handed the gold medal, and friends and family gather round to celebrate your achievement, but you can't help feeling like a fraud, because you know you've done nothing to deserve their praise.

The joy we experience when we win a race or contest comes, not only from beating the other contestants but also from overcoming resistance. Winning stops being fun when there's no effort involved. Take away the challenge from any activity, and it will stop being as satisfying. We obviously don't want too many obstacles, lest we become frustrated and embittered, but obstacles and challenges do have a place in life, just as gravity and friction do. Therefore, we mustn't despise them, neither must we allow ourselves to be frustrated when we encounter these difficulties. With the right attitude, we'll overcome the challenges, and this will also make us a better and more effective person.

Key facts:

- Great accomplishments don't always meet with great approval
- Obstacles, challenges and resistance are a fact of life
- Resistance is the result of activity or progress
- Overcoming resistance can make you a better person
- You can improve your skills by overcoming obstacles
- Overcoming resistance makes us more resilient

Food for thought:

- How have you been approaching your challenges? Have you been getting frustrated with them?
- Are you quick to abandon your plans when you encounter obstacles?

Chapter 19

Winning attitudes

As we edge closer to the end of the book, I'd like to draw your attention to what I consider to be the ultimate ingredient for success. You may have all the knowledge, skills and resources in the world, but if you lack the right mentality, then you may not be able to fulfil your purpose. Having the right attitude brings everything else together. Now, let's take a look at a few of the characteristics that make up *the right attitude*.

A solid work ethic

Every problem can be overcome with the right level of application. No problem can withstand the power of persistence. You can split boulders into small pieces of rock with nothing but a hammer and a chisel if you keep at it long enough and apply the right amount of force. A tree can be felled with an axe just as well as with a chainsaw—you've just got to work a bit harder. Likewise, you can get anything you want from life and overcome every obstacle if you keep chipping away at it.

Most people want success, but very few are prepared to work hard for it. As soon as they hear the word "work", their eyes glaze over. They want to be successful but without applying themselves, and that's nothing but self-deception. If you really want to be successful, you have to love work. If you don't believe it, ask any self-made millionaire—they'll tell you that they don't merely believe in working hard, but they also love to work. Every successful person knows this. You need to stop seeing work as a painful necessity or even as a curse. Stop singing: "Thank God it's Friday"!

Work is by no means a curse. It is through work that the earth was formed, and every productive activity on earth involves work. So leave behind the fantasy of wanting success without treading the path towards it. Don't love sleep too much if you want to be successful. Let sleep serve a purpose. Treat it as a resource. Don't sleep for 10 hours just because it's nighttime—remember that you have only 24 hours in a day, some of which will be taken up by other activities, including unplanned ones. Sleep enough to regenerate your strength and then get up and work!

> Do not love sleep or you will grow poor; stay awake, and
> you will have food to spare.

> Solomon (Proverbs 20:13 NIV)

When I was in school, there was this chap who was often top in the exams, although he was only a little above average when we all started. I remember scoring higher marks than him in the earlier years—but he had a secret that would help him all the way to the top. That secret was *diligence*. He'd spend hours studying, and he'd ask question after question in class. Sometimes, he'd hold up the lesson, which made him unpopular; but he was only making sure that he'd understood what had been taught. His attitude paid off when he was among those with the best results in the school, as well as in the entire country. How did he do that? Through hard work!

So, why don't you get off your backside and get stuck in? Don't sit back and expect life to hand you something for free. Life owes you nothing if you don't work hard. If you do work hard though, you'll reap the results!

Can-do attitude

One player I admire in the world of tennis is Simona Halep, a Romanian professional tennis player. Measuring 1.68 meters, she's not the tallest player in the women's game, and height is important in tennis. But her short stature doesn't stop her featuring consistently in the top 10 of the Women's Tennis Association rankings.

Unlike Serena Williams, Maria Sharapova or Angelique Kerber; Halep isn't big on hitting. But, her tenacity, can-do attitude and sheer determination more than make up for her lack of power. In 2017 she rose to number one in the WTA rankings, going past the likes of Pliskova, Angelique Kerber, Garbine Muguruza and Caroline Wozniacki—all of whom are taller and better servers than she is. How did she do it? Through sheer determination!

Playing against Halep must feel like playing against a wall. It doesn't matter how hard her opponent hits the ball, Halep manages to return it. In the 2017 French Open, I saw her play against Jelena Ostapenko. Ostapenko was the new kid on the block and with all the power in the world as well as plenty of on-court tenacity, she gave everyone a fright, except for Halep that is. She stood her ground and put up a fight. Ostapenko won that match, as in the end, her power proved too much, but she certainly had to earn her win because Halep gave her the match of her life.

In a world where many are quick to throw in the towel, Halep digs in her heels and refuses to budge. I admire that attitude in people. I just love people who refuse to be intimidated by those who are seemingly more talented or more powerful than them. These for me are the true winners, and if you can master that kind of attitude, then life will have to hand you something. Your talent will be a bonus.

Many people complain about life being unfair, but I look at someone like Halep and think they're wrong. Life *is* fair. Whatever you lack in stature or strength, you can make up for by working harder. Many naturally gifted people don't put in as much work. They get used to things being handed to them on a silver platter, and the world bowing to their excellence. Many were hailed at 16 as the next big stars, but by the time they were 20, they'd fallen by the wayside. They hadn't really applied themselves. They started reading their own press releases and began to relax too much. They thought success would keep coming just because they were talented. They didn't know that the new definition of talent is hard work.

On the other hand, those who are less naturally gifted know they need to make up for it. They know that life won't hand them anything if they don't apply themselves, and through their hard work, they often get past others that are apparently more gifted.

The new definition of talent is hard work.

Don't stop, keep going

It's fun to watch someone play a sport or perform an art with flair and mastery. In this regard, it doesn't get any better than tennis ace Roger Federer. At 36, Federer has just won his 20th Grand Slam, brushing aside much younger players. It's one thing winning tournaments, but to combine industry with artistry as he does, is sheer brilliance. Federer majestically floats around the court as he dispatches opponent after opponent. One really feels privileged to watch him play.

But as much as I love watching Federer, I'm most inspired by Novak Djokovic. He may not be as artistic as Federer, but he's someone who doesn't know when he's beaten. When I first saw him play in 2005, I immediately knew there was something special about him. He was playing against an evenly matched opponent, and though he had the upper hand, he didn't seem to have the firepower to seal the victory. Instead, he simply hung on until he'd worn his opponent out.

Looking at Djokovic helps me understand another philosophy of life: if you hang in there long enough, you'll get something. The vast majority of people will have a go at something for a day or a week, and if they really push themselves, they'll keep going for a month, but then they've had it. They lack stamina. But if you want to win something in life, you have to get stuck in. You just have to keep going.

Never say die

Djokovic was nowhere near the top of the ATP rankings when the likes of Roger Federer and Rafa Nadal were ruling the roost, but that didn't stop him from inviting himself to the party.

He announced himself to the world at the 2008 Australian Open, beating whoever needed beating to lift the trophy at the tender age of 20. He seemed to fade for a little after that, but he was back again in 2011 to wreak more havoc. That year, he beat the almost indomitable Nadal in 6 separate finals, winning 3 Grand Slams in the process, and taking the number one spot in the world rankings from him.

Unbeaten for a run of 43 matches, Djokovic caused rampage wherever he went; that is until he was called to order at Roland Garos by none other than King Roger himself. The most remarkable thing about this achievement is that Djokovic did it with little support from tennis fans. To this day there are far more Roger Federer and Rafa Nadal fans than there are Djokovic fans. He often plays in front of crowds that will not cheer him on, but that doesn't stop him from excelling.

During a US Open semi-final against Federer, Djokovic endured constant onslaught from a crowd that was determined to see only one person win that competition, and they nearly succeeded. Federer came within a whisker of the final, but he was playing against a guy who refused to be beaten.

Federer was 40-15 up and serving for the match when Djokovic gave him the return of his life. This rattled Roger, and what ensued was testimony to Djokovic's never-say-die attitude. He went on to win the match in 5 sets, and eventually the competition; proving that sometimes all you need to do is refuse to be beaten. Also noteworthy was his refusal to feel sorry for himself—many would have lost that match for the lack of support alone.

In his post-match interview, Djokovic had this to say: "I was very close to being on my way back home... it's always important to be calm, to stay positive, and to believe, to believe that you can win." Now, that's what I call a winning attitude! If you want to win in life, you need to adopt this attitude too; and remember that you must never feel sorry for yourself.

Dare to question the status quo

I like the Biblical story of Gideon because it is the ultimate display of a winning attitude. Gideon was the son of a man named Joash of the Israelite tribe of Manasseh. An Abiezerite, Gideon belonged to one of the least-esteemed clans of the 12 tribes of Israel. He was no one's hero.

When Gideon was hiding in a cave, an angel appeared to him. These were troubling times, and the nation was being plundered systematically by Midianites who would arrive promptly at harvest to loot much of the crop and damage the rest. People had to hide their farm produce in caves to keep it safe from the looters. No one felt able to address this intolerable situation. Gideon felt powerless too, but it seems that he'd been turning the matter over in his mind, so when the angel appeared, Gideon had a question for him.

"The Lord is with you, mighty warrior", said the angel as a greeting.

"O my lord, if the Lord is with us, why then has all this happened to us?" replied Gideon.

Gideon seemed to be questioning the angel, which seems surprising. Angelic visitations were rare even then, and those who experienced them were usually very afraid. Questioning an angel was unthinkable, but Gideon was quite unlike other people.

It's worth noting the point that Gideon was making. Here he was, hiding from the enemy in a cave. How could anyone consider him a warrior? Besides, if God was indeed with *him,* and by implication, the whole nation, then why had He (God) not done anything about the situation? Such were the questions on Gideon's mind.

The angel was pleased: "Go in this strength of yours and you'll conquer the Midianites", he said.

We might all ask: what strength this was. Here was a man hiding from his enemies in a cave—what strength had Gideon displayed? But it seems that the angel could see something in him that others, including Gideon himself, couldn't. Following this event, Gideon went on to defeat thousands of Midianites with an army of just 300 men. There was strength in that questioning attitude, and that's the sort of attitude we need today.

Far too many people go through life passively, without asking any questions or challenging the status quo. Some are stuck in dead-end jobs with no prospect of personal or professional development. They barely make ends meet, but they're too scared to ask questions. Others have dreams that could change the world, but they haven't managed to get anything going, and don't want to rock the boat. They've switched on cruise control and are coasting along to retirement, even though they know this isn't their true destiny.

Many of us have stopped asking questions, and that's the reason our situations haven't changed. It's also the reason that so many of the world's problems remain unresolved.

Whenever there's a natural disaster, people ask, "Where is God?" We seem to expect the solution to our problems to come from beyond our planet. But I would rather ask, "What are *you* going to do about it?" We're the ones that live here. We are the managers of the earth, and it's our responsibility, not God's, to sort out the world's problems,. This is why we need enquiring minds, but we need to ask *ourselves,* not God, the questions. If you're unhappy about your situation, then start asking questions about how you can change it. Don't be passive; act! If you start asking questions, you may unearth hidden strengths. Gideon had in him the strength to tackle his and the nation's problems, but he only discovered this strength by asking the right questions.

Relentlessness

During the battle, Gideon displayed another important virtue: perseverance. The enemy had fled the battle scene, but instead of declaring victory, Gideon and his men chased them beyond the country's borders and completely defeated them. Had they not done so, the Midianites would have returned the following year.

The biblical account states that Gideon kept going even when he was exhausted. Now that's a winning attitude. Gideon didn't stop, and neither should you. Many people will pursue a cause until they come across an obstacle, score a small victory or until such a time as abandoning it seems justifiable. Gideon was different—he kept going until victory was complete. Once you adopt this attitude, you'll be a winner.

Losing attitudes

Just as having the right mentality brings success, having the wrong one leads to failure. Here are a few examples of losing attitudes:

A sense of entitlement

A sense of entitlement is one of the reasons that some people don't want to work very hard. They think life owes them something. This attitude is rife in western societies that have good social welfare systems. These systems often lead people to believe that the state owes them something, and they get upset if they don't get what they think they deserve. But the truth is that no one owes you anything. If you want something, go and get it! Put in the effort. A sense of entitlement is a losing attitude, and it often leads on to the one that follows:

Playing the blame game

The world is not a perfect place, and sometimes bad things happen. When they do, having the right attitude can get us through. But many people struggle with this; they often think it must be someone's fault that things aren't going their way, and so they look for someone to blame.

Playing the blame game will only distract you from finding a solution to your problem. Your situation may well be a direct consequence of someone's actions, but focusing on that isn't going to help you find a solution. Besides, regardless of what has happened, you need to find a way out, so why not focus on that instead.

Complacency

Earlier on, we mentioned how readiness to work hard and to persevere is part of a winning attitude. The direct opposites, one could say, are complacency and laziness. The complacent part of us says: "I've worked hard enough. Now I can sit back and enjoy the fruits of my labour." It's great to celebrate your achievements with friends and family, but sitting back for an indefinite period to glory in your minor accomplishments is a killer. That's the reason that many sportsmen and women just fade away after one major victory. It's best to avoid these complacency breaks, as they're difficult to come back from.

Key facts:

- To succeed in life, you need a solid work ethic
- It pays to work hard
- If you stick at something long enough, you'll be rewarded
- A questioning mind is a sign of strength
- A sense of entitlement is a killer
- Don't blame others for your problems, but focus on the solution instead
- Don't take complacency breaks, or you'll have a hard time making your way back to the top

Chapter 20

Time to arise

Thank you for coming with me on this journey thus far. We began by introducing you to two people facing a crisis and concluded that they both needed an appraisal.

We also noted that it was essential, especially for Andy, that his appraisal was thorough. He really needs to dig deep to discover his true destiny because it's far from obvious. After all, Andy has lived a meaningful life, having achieved what most people aim for: a successful career and a happy family.

Besides, the call for an appraisal isn't a call to measure your accomplishments against the achievements of others, but a call to judge your achievements against your purpose. You may have accomplished a lot, but in comparison to what you've been destined to do—you may well have underachieved.

Moreover, Andy cannot escape an in-depth appraisal. If he doesn't have one now or chooses to have only a superficial one, the need for a proper appraisal will become even more pressing later. No one can escape a thorough appraisal at some point in life, regardless of how rich or poor they are. Whether you live in the third world or the first world, you won't be able to escape it. You may think you can break the rules, but unless death comes unexpectedly, you will have an appraisal before you make your final bow. Alone on your deathbed, the questions you have been avoiding will appear again. One of those questions will be: "What will I be remembered for?"

You'll also feel regret. Will you regret having done too much or too little? Will you be concerned about having made a fool of yourself while trying to help someone, or that you let your hang-ups get in the way of doing what's right? Will you be sorry that you didn't go on as many holidays as you'd have liked, that you hadn't built a bigger house for yourself, or driven a more luxurious car? Or, will you be sorry that you didn't help enough people with the resources you had?

One day, when you're lying on your deathbed wondering how you've spent your time on earth, you won't regret having done too much. Instead, you'll be sad that you didn't do more. In that critical moment, you'll know that a fear of failure was a poor excuse for failing to fulfil your potential.

It's not too late

You may have lived a horrible life up to this point. Like Sarah, you may be sitting in a prison cell at this very moment. Your life up to this point may have been one big catalogue of errors, but that doesn't matter. It doesn't matter what mistakes you've made, I don't care if you've perpetrated the most atrocious acts—you still have an assignment that only you can fulfil.

Your crimes, evil deeds and stupidity may have taken you off-course, but you can still change direction and start working your way towards your real destiny. You don't have to live up to the labels that your misdeeds have given you. You have an assignment that only you can fulfil, so shake off the shame and stigma, and apply the principles you've learned from this book—you can then start to turn your life around! Your life doesn't need to be like a broken record as you keep repeating the same mistakes again and again. Don't let negative thoughts keep you from acting—your assignment is too important!

Conversely, you may have lived what appears to others to have been a meaningful life. Perhaps, like Andy, you've already reached the height of your career. You may have a good job, a handsome salary, a happy family, and a great pension to look forward to. Life may have treated you well, but deep down you know there's more. You know you haven't harnessed even half of your potential, and that there are dreams trapped inside you waiting to manifest. So, what are you going to do? Will you find yourself a new hobby to keep you going, and just forget about the questions we asked earlier? Are you just going to sit there paralysed with the fear of failure?

Arise and be someone's deliverer!

I like the story of the three lepers of Samaria. Their city had been besieged by enemy forces for months, and so no one could enter or leave. The food had run out, and people were dying of starvation. The situation was so bad that people had resorted to cannibalism. The three lepers, who were sitting at the city gate, said to one another: "How long will we sit here for; until we die? Arise now! Let's go over to the enemy camp. If they kill us, we will but die, but if they don't, then we will live."

Let me explain their logic. There was no food in the city or at the city gates, but the lepers knew there would be some in the enemy camp. Off they went, surely to their death, one would think. When they arrived at the enemy camp, however, they found it deserted. The enemy had fled after hearing noises that had sounded like an attack. But no one in the city knew about it because they'd been too frightened to step outside the city walls.

That day, the three lepers, formerly shunned by society because of their illness, became national heroes as they returned to inform the inhabitants of what they'd seen. There was great rejoicing once they'd obtained supplies from outside, and everyone ate their fill.

If they hadn't dared to act, the three lepers, along with everyone else, in Samaria would have starved to death. Likewise, your own destiny is tied to that of others. The day you decide to change something in your life, you'll not only set yourself free, but you'll also bring relief to many other people. Many will rise up and follow your example as your actions will have emboldened them. So will you arise today and be someone's deliverer?

A decision to act is worth more than a thousand ideas.

Arise and act, and leave your mark in the world

We've all made our appearance on earth that we might leave a legacy behind. The world we now live in didn't just happen—someone conceived the idea of vehicles, and built them; someone else thought of roads and built them. Bill Gates wanted to see a computer in every home and developed software to make it possible. And someone else created computer hardware. Such people have made a big difference in our lives. Their vision, foresight and determination to succeed are the reasons for the many conveniences we enjoy today.

Some lived to enjoy the fruit of their labours, while others toiled, not knowing whether they would ever see their efforts rewarded. But they've left their indelible mark on our lives nonetheless. We cannot forget Steve Jobs, George Washington Carver, Nelson Mandela or Mahatma Gandhi, alongside many others who have helped to make the world what it is today.

Such are the dreamers who break away from the tyranny of the present and stretch their necks out into the future to bring us new inventions and other kinds of benefits. Additionally, we should also remember the visionaries alive today, whose actions give us a reason to believe that we too can make our mark.

We rightly call them heroes, but such people don't really think of themselves as such. As far as they're concerned, they've merely answered the call of destiny in the legacies they've left behind. That's why you should never ignore the calls from within your soul. There's a reason for you feeling unsettled, even when you have sufficient funds in the bank to ease your tension. Destiny is calling out to you to rise above your circumstances and leave behind your legacy. So, what are you going to do? Will you sit down for that appraisal while you still have the time?

There are three stages in life: morning, afternoon and evening. The *morning stage* is when we prepare the ground for what lies ahead. For most of us, this is when we go to school and start a career. We often have little control over what happens to us in this stage, as our parents and the education system call the shots. But there's also an *afternoon stage*, by which time most of us are working, have started a family and are seemingly masters of our own destiny. It is at this stage that we get the chance to think about the question of legacy. Very few of us will be lucky enough to consider these issues in the morning stage of our lives. If what you've read in this book resonates, then you're either an extremely reflective person, or you're in the afternoon or evening stage of your life. You haven't got much time left, you know.

You may think of yourself as being too small or insignificant to leave a mark on humanity, but you're underestimating the power within you. Every tree begins as a seed, and given the right conditions, it breaks through the ground and begins its upward journey. Day after day it toils relentlessly until it joins the canopy of the forest, and after years of toil, the tree fulfils its purpose in the world—to provide shade and sustenance for all. And you my friend, if only you will recognise and develop the potential within you, are also like a mighty tree waiting to mature.

So, will you arise and take action? Will you harness the power of your dreams, discover your resources, and chart a path for a better future for yourself and for others? Or do you prefer instead to sit there and rue your mistakes and missed opportunities? As the lepers of Samaria asked each other, so I ask you; how long will you sit there for? Until you die? One day you'll look back and regret that you didn't take action. Arise now and lay the foundation for a better future—only you can do it. Arise and live for something bigger than yourself! Arise out of your "meaningful life" and live for your true purpose instead!.

References

1. Quotes from Newton: https://fromthelighthouseblog.wordpress.com/2013/02/11/thinking-continuosly-how-adopting-isaac-newtons-approach-would-improve-your-business/

2. *What's the purpose of life – 16 Possible Answers From 16 Inspirational People*: http://www.finerminds.com/happiness/whats-the-purpose-of-life-16-possible-answers-from-16-inspirational-people/

3. "Top 40 signs of having a midlife crisis revealed": http://www.telegraph.co.uk/news/newstopics/howaboutthat/10156725/Top-40-signs-of-a-midlife-crisis-revealed.html

4. "Famous people on the meaning of life": http://www.preachingtoday.com/illustrations/2011/july/2070411.html

5. French Open 2014: "How a breast reduction helped Simona Halep unleash her full potential": http://www.telegraph.co.uk/sport/tennis/frenchopen/10861164/French-Open-2014-How-a-breast-reduction-helped-Simona-Halep-unleash-her-full-potential.html

6. "Longest match-winning streaks in professional tennis from 1975 to 2017": https://www.statista.com/statistics/276898/longest-winning-streaks-in-professional-tennis/

7. US Open 2011: "Roger Federer struggles to accept Novak Djokovic defeat": https://www.theguardian.com/sport/2011/sep/11/us-open-2011-federer-djokovic

8. "Midlife crisis":
   http://research.omicsgroup.org/index.php/Midlife_crisishttp://
   research.omicsgroup.org/index.php/Midlife_crisis

9. Elliott Jaques: "Analysing business, the army and our midlife crises":
   https://www.theguardian.com/education/2003/apr/11/higher
   education.uk1

10. *Stop working for **uncle Sam*, Dr Sunday Adelaja

11. *The Pursuit of Purpose*, Dr Myles Munroe

12. *Who am I, why am I here?* Dr Sunday Adelaja

13. *How to become great through time conversion*, Dr Sunday Adelaja

14. "7 Signs You Might Be Facing A Midlife Crisis"
    https://www.huffingtonpost.co.uk/entry/midlife-crisis_n_4419481

15. "Thai cave rescue: How the boys were saved":
    https://www.bbc.co.uk/news/world-asia-44695232

16. "Broken Hearts and Deal Breakers: Reasons Why People Divorce":
    https://www.psychologytoday.com/gb/blog/sliding-vs-deciding/
    201704/broken-hearts-and-deal-breakers-reasons-why-people-
    divorce

17. "The Transtheoretical Model" https://www.prochange.com/trans
    theoretical-model-of-behavior-change

18. https://www.prochange.com/transtheoretical-model-of-
    behavior-change

19. *Living Forward*, Michael Hyatt and Daniel Harkavy

20. *Your best year every*, Michael Hyatt

21. *Half Time*, Bob Buford

22. *Game Plan*, Bob Buford

23. *Problems, your shortcut to prominence*, Sunday Adelaja

24. *Start Now Get Perfect Later*, Rob Moore

About the Author

Dr Ben Quartsin is a Consultant psychiatrist based in the United Kingdom.

On completion of his secondary education in Ghana, he travelled to Poland where he obtained a medical degree from Wroclaw Medical University. This training gave him the opportunity to interact with people from all over the world.

Following his successful time in Poland, Dr Quartsin continued his postgraduate training in the United Kingdom where he currently practices with a special interest in psychopathology and psychological treatments.

Beyond psychiatry, Dr Quartsin takes a keen interest in personal development and understanding human behaviour, including the factors that influence our choices. He is genuinely passionate about unleashing human potential.

Dr Quartsin currently resides in Hampshire with his family, where he enjoys cycling and going for walks in the countryside.

Printed in the United States
By Bookmasters